THE BOOK OF
IRISH SPORTING HEROES

ADRIAN RUSSELL

ILLUSTRATED BY
GRAHAM CORCORAN

RED SHED

ADRIAN RUSSELL is the Digital Sports Editor of the *Irish Examiner*. He was previously the author of *The Double: How Cork Made GAA History*. He plays five-a-side football with his friends and helps train Glen Rovers' U6 camogie team. He lives in Cork with his wife Sara and daughters, Robin and Ruby.

GRAHAM CORCORAN is an award-winning illustrator specializing in creating children's book art, as well as pop-culture poster art which he has exhibited internationally. With over 20 years experience, he has developed his signature style from a love of retro mid-century illustration combined with modern themes. Graham lives in Dublin with his wife Nicole.

CONTENTS

INTRODUCTION	4
A HISTORY OF SOCCER IN IRELAND	6
IRISH INTERNATIONAL SOCCER	8
IRISH PLAYERS AROUND THE WORLD	12
TOP IRISH PLAYERS OF ALL TIME	14
IRISH WOMEN'S FOOTBALL	16
SOCCER AT HOME AND THE LEAGUE OF IRELAND	18
A HISTORY OF THE GAA	20
HURLING AND CAMOGIE	22
GAELIC FOOTBALL	24
OUR OTHER GAMES	26
THE GREATEST HURLING AND CAMOGIE PLAYERS OF ALL TIME	28
THE GREATEST GAELIC FOOTBALLERS OF ALL TIME	30
CROKE PARK	34
THE AVIVA	35
A HISTORY OF RUGBY IN IRELAND	36
THE FOUR PROVINCES	38
IRISH INTERNATIONAL RUGBY	40
IRISH WOMEN'S RUGBY	42
GREATEST IRISH RUGBY PLAYERS	46
A HISTORY OF BOXING IN IRELAND	48
HALL OF FAME	50
IRELAND'S GREATEST BOXING MOMENTS	52
A HISTORY OF HORSE RACING IN IRELAND	54
THE GREATEST IRISH HORSES	56
GREATEST IRISH JOCKEYS AND TRAINERS	58
IRELAND AND THE OLYMPICS	60
ATHLETICS	62
IRISH ATHLETES ACROSS THE OLYMPICS	64
THE PARALYMPICS	66
OLYMPIC AQUATICS & THE SPECIAL OLYMPICS	68
GREAT OLYMPIC MOMENTS	70
CYCLING	72
SPORTING PIONEERS	74
RISING STARS	76–9
A HISTORY OF GOLF IN IRELAND	80
BEST IRISH GOLFERS	82
SNOOKER AND DARTS	84
THE WIDER WORLD OF SPORT	86
FACTS	88
QUIZ & ANSWERS	90
INDEX	92

INTRODUCTION

Ireland might be a small island, but we punch well above our weight when it comes to sport. From the humble origins of today's professional and elite amateur sports, our athletes have gone on to play and win in the biggest tournaments, exciting audiences around the world with their skill and changing the way sports are played around the world.

This book looks to tell the story of Irish sport through the achievements of our incredible athletes. Some of them reached the top of their game, others influenced their sport or overcame huge challenges. All of them have inspirational stories to tell, which hopefully help us to better understand our country and ourselves.

Over the course of this book you'll get to learn about and cheer on some of our Irish sporting heroes: the boxers who've punched their way to Olympic gold, the Irish footballers who've taken on the best in the game as well as talented and brave athletes who've helped blaze a trail for those who follow. And you'll also get an introduction to some of the next generation of Irish sports stars likely to light up our screens in the years to come.

It was an almost impossible job to pick the people we'd include in this book. For every sports star we selected for our team, there were many, many more whose stories are definitely worth including too. Squeezing in as much as we did between the covers was very difficult and we had lots of fun arguments.

Maybe you think we've forgotten someone? You should certainly tell the author when you see him on the street. In the meantime, there's a section at the back of this book for you to write the story of your favourite sporting hero.

And hopefully this book will be just the beginning, as you learn about our sports history and explore even more of the people who've represented us on tracks and pitches throughout the years.

By the time you get to the end of this book, we hope you'll know a bit more about the people who've defined Irish sport so far. As well as being a lot more useful in quizzes, maybe you'll also be inspired to try to run faster than our sprinters, win more All-Irelands than our record-breaking GAA stars, or perhaps you'll want to try a new sport and just maybe add your part to our brilliant sporting history.

On your marks, get set …

ADRIAN RUSSELL

A HISTORY OF SOCCER IN IRELAND

Football is the world's game. And we love to play and watch it here in Ireland too.

We like soccer so much that electricity suppliers have to prepare for a surge in demand for power during big games like World Cup finals. Why? Because so many of us run to the kitchen to put the kettle on for a nice pot of tea at half-time.

Our international teams have made their mark on the biggest stage, our fans have cheered on our teams across the globe, and we have clubs with long, proud traditions. It's one of the most popular sports to play for Irish people – from five-a-side games to lots of local leagues.

DID YOU KNOW?
Ireland might be famous for playing in green, but we actually started out in 'St Patrick's blue' against Bulgaria at the 1924 Paris Olympics, for our first official match as the Republic of Ireland.

BUT WHEN DOES FOOTBALL'S STORY IN IRELAND BEGIN?

Well, it starts with a love story, funnily enough.

We have to go back to 1878 when Belfast businessman John McAlery saw an organised football game for the first time while on honeymoon in Edinburgh. 'What is this game?' he asked his bride.

The official rules of the new sport had been agreed in 1863, when the Football Association was created in England. McAlery enjoyed the game so much, he invited some Scottish football teams to Belfast to play an exhibition. Soon the game became more and more popular – in the north of the island especially.

The Irish Football Association (IFA) was then founded in Belfast in 1880 and for over 40 years it organised the game for all of Ireland. But soon there was a row – and it wouldn't be the last one in Irish football. The massive political events of the time meant that Ireland would be split into two – Northern Ireland and the Republic of Ireland – and how football was organised here would also be divided.

Some clubs in Dublin withdrew from the IFA's league. A disagreement between Glenavon and Shelbourne about the location for a cup replay led to the Football Association of Ireland (FAI) being formed in an historic meeting in Dublin in June 1921.

The League of Ireland was formed for clubs in the south and in 1922 when the FAI joined FIFA, the Republic of Ireland could field a team against the other nations of the world.

FIRST IRISH INTERNATIONAL SOCCER MATCH

Before the split between the IFA and the FAI, Ireland lost their first international football game 13-0 to England. It remains our worst ever defeat!

The game was played in front of around 2,500 people at Blackpool's Bloomfield Park in England in February 1882.

A few days later, Ireland played their second-ever game – this time losing to Wales 7-1. We were already getting better, right? Sammy Johnson scored the goal – our first ever at international level.

Later, the Republic of Ireland's first game saw the so-called Irish Free State team compete in the 1924 Paris Olympics.

JACK KIRWAN

Ajax, based in Amsterdam in the Netherlands, is one of the most successful football clubs in the world – and their first 'professional' manager was an Irishman called Jack Kirwan.

Born in 1878, Kirwan carved out a great career in England with teams like Spurs, Chelsea and Everton. After his retirement, a chance meeting saw the Wicklow man take over Ajax, who had never won anything and didn't even play in the top Dutch division.

The Irishman had *lots* of ideas about training and playing and he brought Ajax to the top division in 1911. Jack left the Netherlands in 1915 after the outbreak of World War I. He went on to manage Irish side Bohemians. When he was struggling later in life, the members of Ajax came together to help their former hero.

OSCAR TRAYNOR

For many years soccer was considered a 'foreign game' in Ireland – the GAA even banned their members from playing it. Oscar Traynor stood up for the sport and helped it grow here.

Born in 1886 in Dublin, Traynor grew up to become an important member of Ireland's revolutionary generation. He fought in the 1916 Rising, was a leader in the War of Independence and took the anti-Treaty side in the Civil War. Later he was elected to the Dáil and was minister of defence during World War II, or 'The Emergency' as it was called here.

In 1948 he became president of the FAI and remained so until he died in 1963. During that time he spoke out for the 'foreign game' here and insisted Irish people should play and watch any sport they want. The Oscar Traynor Cup is played in his honour today.

IRISH INTERNATIONAL SOCCER

Stand up if… you want to learn about the Boys in Green!

The Republic of Ireland football team is known for playing hard, having great supporters and sometimes pulling off big results as underdogs.

Ireland play their home games at the Aviva Stadium in Dublin, which was known as Lansdowne Road before it was redeveloped in 2010. The FAI share the stadium with Ireland's rugby team – the goalposts are changed and the pitch lines are repainted when needed. The stadium holds 52,000 people and is often full of football fans chanting and singing songs like 'Olé Olé Olé Olé' and 'Stand Up for the Boys in Green' at big games.

FUN FACT
'THE GRANNY RULE'
Ireland has had lots of brilliant players through the years thanks to the so-called Granny Rule. FIFA allow players to declare for a country of their parents' birth or where their grandparents came from. Which international teams could you play for?

LIAM WHELAN

William – or Billy or Liam – Whelan signed for the famous Manchester United as an 18-year-old in 1953. He had caught the eye of manager Matt Busby while playing for Home Farm in his hometown of Dublin. He scored 52 goals in 98 games for the exciting young side that became known as the 'Busby Babes'.

The team never fulfilled their massive potential, tragically. Their plane crashed on the runway in Munich, Germany, on the way back from a European Cup tie in 1958. Whelan was one of 20 people, including 8 players, who died in the Munich air disaster. A bridge near Liam's home in Phibsboro was named after him and unveiled by his former teammate Bobby Charlton in 2005.

RAY HOUGHTON

'Who put the ball in the English net?' Ray Houghton is the answer to this famous Irish chant because he scored Ireland's first-ever goal at a major championship. Not the tallest player, Houghton leapt highest to head the winner against England at Euro '88 in Stuttgart. The creative midfielder won the old First Division – before the English Premier League existed – with Liverpool. He went on to score the winner against Italy at the World Cup in USA '94. He was born in Glasgow, Scotland but decided to play for his father's country. Lucky us.

NIALL QUINN

The Mighty Quinn did it all. The tall Dubliner played in an All-Ireland minor hurling final before making a name for himself with Arsenal. Showing off his Gaelic football skills, he once scored a goal for Man City before then saving a penalty in the same game after their keeper was sent off. Quinn scored a crucial World Cup goal for Ireland at Italia '90 against the Netherlands. After he finished playing, he became manager, part-owner and chairman of Sunderland. Phew!

IRISH FANS

Irish football supporters are known for their passionate support of our team, having fun and not causing trouble. They've helped change car tyres in foreign cities, sung lullabies to babies, cleaned up town squares and turned up in huge numbers to back our teams.

BRAGGING RIGHTS

In the early days of international football, England were the best around and had never lost a home game to a 'foreign team'. In 1949, however, the Republic of Ireland travelled to Everton's Goodison Park and won 2-0 to make history. Payback for our 13-0 defeat all those years before!

NORTHERN IRELAND

Northern Ireland, who play their home games at Windsor Park in Belfast, have made a big impression on the football world despite the nation's small size.

Long before the Republic of Ireland got there, Northern Ireland competed at the 1958 World Cup, getting to the quarter-finals. They were captained by Danny Blanchflower, who is regarded as one of Tottenham's greatest ever players.

The Green and White Army saw their team play in the 1982 World Cup, where they beat hosts Spain. Norman Whiteside made his debut at the tournament at 17 years old, becoming the youngest player ever to feature at a World Cup – a record that still stands today. How long until you're 17 and playing at a World Cup?

Northern Ireland also got to the 1986 World Cup in Mexico and its first ever Euros in France in 2016, where they reached the round of 16. Just imagine if we joined forces.

☆ GOLDEN AGES ☆
THE CHARLTON YEARS

FUN FACT
Bobby and Jack are one of just two sets of brothers to win the World Cup. The others were West Germany's Fritz and Ottmar Walter in 1954.

FUN FACT
Olé Olé Olé Olé! The Irish team recorded their official anthem for the 1990 World Cup called 'Put 'Em Under Pressure'. It was No. 1 in the charts for 13 weeks!

Ireland had lots of excellent players and great teams through the years but we had never managed to qualify for the World Cup. All that changed after Jack Charlton became Republic of Ireland manager in 1986.

As a player, 'Big Jack' starred for Leeds United and won a World Cup as a centre back for England in 1966, playing alongside his little brother Bobby.

Charlton was an experienced manager and promised that Ireland would be successful. He wasn't very good at remembering the players' names, but he recognised they were an excellent squad.

FUN FACT
Before the quarter-final, Charlton took the squad to visit the pope in the Vatican in Rome. Pope John Paul II, who was a goalkeeper in his youth, wished them luck, especially Packie Bonner.

ITALIA '90

Two years later Irish supporters were headed for our first World Cup, Italia '90. Ireland did brilliantly and got to the knock-out stages. The Boys in Green played out a scoreless draw with Romania and the game went to a dramatic penalty shootout.

Packie Bonner saved Romania's fourth kick and centre back David O'Leary – who'd never taken a penalty before – walked up to take the crucial spotter. If he scored, Ireland would be in the quarter-final of a World Cup.

FUN FACT
An estimated half a million people turned up in Dublin to welcome home the Irish squad after Italia '90. It was a massive party!

David smashed the penalty home, all his teammates ran onto the pitch and jumped on him in a massive huddle.

EUROS

Playing a direct style of football, Ireland battled their way to Euro '88 – our very first major tournament. Our first game was against neighbours England. Ireland were underdogs but were ready for the occasion. Ray Houghton scored in the first half and Jack Charlton's men held out for the win. The stadium went mad!

We were eventually knocked out by the Netherlands after an amazing performance in the tournament.

A few days later Ireland played the hosts Italy, one of the best teams in the world. It was the end of an amazing adventure for Ireland, who lost 1-0 thanks to a goal from the tournament's star striker, Toto Schillaci.

'A nation holds its breath!'
– GEORGE HAMILTON

☆ GOLDEN AGES ☆

THE MICK MCCARTHY ERA

FUN FACT

WHO ARE IRELAND'S TOP SCORERS EVER?
Robbie Keane **68**
Niall Quinn **21**
Frank Stapleton **20**

When Charlton left the Ireland job after an amazing decade in charge, his former 'Captain Fantastic', Mick McCarthy, took over in 1996. He modernised the way Ireland played and brought through young players like Damien Duff and Robbie Keane.

In 2001, Ireland had a chance of making it to the World Cup. Holland came to Dublin with a team packed full of superstars. Led by skipper Roy Keane, the Boys in Green managed to shock the Dutch, thanks to a Jason McAteer goal and some brilliant defending. Ireland were on the way back to the World Cup!

SAIPAN

Ireland got to the World Cup, but our best player and captain wouldn't play. Roy Keane would miss out on the World Cup because of a massive argument with his manager.

Before the tournament, Mick McCarthy brought his players to a training camp on a quiet island in the western Pacific, called Saipan. The name would become infamous in Irish sports history. The Man Utd captain, Roy Keane, wasn't very impressed by the training pitch and the conditions at the camp and the argument ended with him leaving the camp. This was headline news in Ireland and beyond. Taoiseach Bertie Ahern even promised to fix the problem. But Ireland continued without their best player.

GERMANY

Robbie Keane would score an amazing 68 goals for Ireland in his career – maybe the most important of them all was against Germany in 2002. Ireland were one goal down against one of the best teams in the world and desperate to equalise.

Cheered on by thousands of fans who'd travelled all the way to Japan, Ireland put Germany under pressure, even though their keeper, Oliver Kahn, was the best in the world.

Then, late in injury time, Niall Quinn cushioned a header down for his strike partner Robbie Keane. The young forward got the ball under control and blasted it past Kahn to send the stadium wild.

Ireland qualified from their group with Germany. In the second round, we gave Spain a massive fright and should have won but went out in a dramatic penalty shootout. It was the end of an amazing, eventful journey.

'Look at these scenes! Just look at the scenes!'
– JOHN MOTSON

IRISH PLAYERS AROUND THE WORLD

ROY KEANE

Roy Keane is one of the icons of the Premier League era, and his sporting story begins in Cork, where he played for Rockmount AFC and then Cobh Ramblers in the League of Ireland. Eventually, he signed for English club Nottingham Forest.

Keane quickly established himself and earned a move to Manchester United, who had just won the first Premier League title in 1993, for a British record transfer fee of £3.75m.

Alex Ferguson strapped the captain's armband on Keane in 1996. He led United to a Champions League win in 1999, getting them to the final thanks to a goal and memorable performance in the semi-final against Italian side Juventus. He had to sit out the dramatic final win over Bayern Munich, though, because he had picked up too many yellow cards. He was pretty fond of tackling!

Keane left Old Trafford after a row with his manager in 2005 (there's a pattern here). He departed as a club legend, having won seven league titles, four FA Cups and that European Cup medal.

FUN FACT

RED CARDS

Richard Dunne has the joint highest number of red cards in Premier League history. He picked up eight dismissals during an otherwise brilliant career.

MOST IRISH PREMIER LEAGUE APPEARANCES

1.	Shay Given	451
2.	John O'Shea	445
3.	Richard Dunne	431
4.	Damien Duff	392
5.	Stephen Carr	377

BROTHER WALFRID

Celtic are arguably the most successful club in Scotland. They were the first British team to win the European Cup in 1967 and their famous ground Parkhead always has an amazing atmosphere. The club has a strong Irish connection.

Did you know the club was founded by an Irish priest called Brother Walfrid? Andrew Kerins was born in Ballymote, Co. Sligo in 1840 and took his new name when he became a Marist Brother.

He was a teacher in Glasgow and London, where he was very kind to people, especially the poor children of immigrants. He decided to set up Celtic Football Club as a way to raise money for the poor.

The club became very important to Irish immigrants who made their homes in Glasgow after the famine. It was successful in raising money for the poor and achieving successes on and off the pitch.

MARTIN O'NEILL

Martin O'Neill managed Celtic during one of their most successful eras. He rebuilt the team and won three titles on the trot as well as getting to a UEFA Cup final. He also played GAA for Derry at Croke Park and got the Republic of Ireland to Euro 2016. Did he also study criminology in college? Guilty, your honour.

TOP IRISH PREMIER LEAGUE SCORERS

1. Robbie Keane — 126
2. Niall Quinn — 59
3. Shane Long — 56
4. Damien Duff — 54
5. Jonathan Walters — 43

LIAM BRADY IN ITALY

Dubliner Liam 'Chippy' Brady earned his nickname because he loved chips, not because of the way he kicked the ball with a sweet left foot. But he did strike it beautifully. The Arsenal star swapped French fries in London for pasta and Italian football in 1980. He went to Turin and won the Serie A title for Juventus with a penalty in the last game of the season. When there weren't many foreign players allowed to play in the league, he starred for Inter Milan, Sampdoria and Ascoli before returning to England. Mamma mia.

DON PATRICIO

Patrick O'Connell was born in Westmeath, grew up in Dublin and went on to captain Manchester United and manage FC Barcelona. When the First World War ended his playing career, he managed Real Betis to the Spanish league title before being lured to the famous Barca.

Again, conflict interrupted Patrick's sporting career. When the Spanish Civil War broke out, football stopped across Spain. 'Don Patricio', as he became known, led his players on a tour of Mexico and the US that brought in lots of money and helped to keep Barcelona alive.

TOP IRISH PLAYERS OF ALL TIME

PAUL MCGRATH

Perhaps the most beloved of all Irish players, McGrath started playing for St Pat's in Dublin. In 1982 he signed for Man Utd where he won major trophies like the FA Cup. After he moved to Aston Villa he won the coveted Player of the Year award in 1993 – the first season of the Premier League.

LIAM BRADY

Liam Brady was a class player from the moment he made his debut for Ireland as a teenager, becoming an Arsenal legend thanks to his wand of a left foot that helped Arsenal to cup glory. He left Highbury and made himself a star in the world's best league in the 1980s, Serie A in Italy. He won a league title or 'scudetto' with Juventus and played for Sampdoria and Inter Milan.

ROBBIE KEANE

If you look up 'striker' in the dictionary, you might just see a picture of Robert David Keane. The Dubliner burst onto the scene as a teenager and scored goals with clubs like Spurs, Liverpool, Leeds, Inter Milan, Celtic and LA Galaxy. Oh, and he's Ireland's top scorer with 68 international strikes. And he had one of the best celebrations in the game. Pew! Pew! Pew!

ROY KEANE

Roy Keane is Ireland's only representative – so far – in the Premier League Hall of Fame. He captained Man Utd and Ireland from midfield and was passionate about everyone always trying their best. He also always stuck up for his teammates and he's remembered as one of the game's best ever players, thanks to his determination to get the most from his talent.

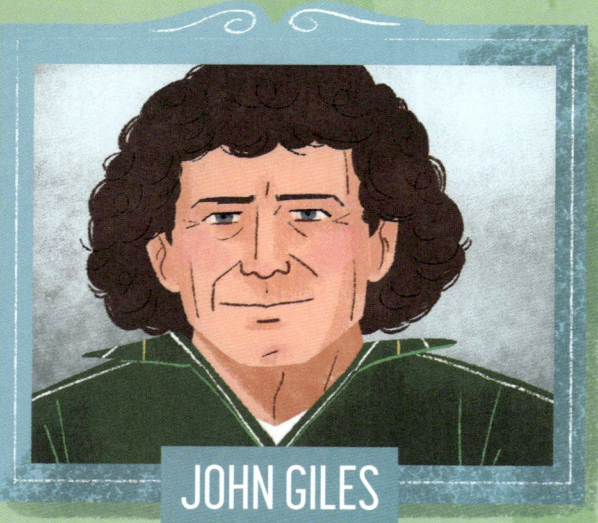

JOHN GILES

With Liam Brady and Eamon Dunphy, John Giles was one of the beloved pundits on RTÉ's soccer panel for many years. But before that, he was a top-class midfielder for Leeds United and Ireland. He won league titles and cups and managed Ireland, where he helped modernise the way the team was organised.

OLIVIA O'TOOLE

Until Robbie Keane took over, Olivia O'Toole was Ireland's record goal scorer. She scored 54 times for her country in 100 caps between 1991 and 2009. Amazingly she won nine league titles and eight FAI Cups!

DAMIEN DUFF

Brian Kerr once said Duffer had adhesive mattress syndrome because it was hard to get the winger out of bed for training. But when the Chelsea and Newcastle star got going he was unstoppable. He won Premier League titles under José Mourinho and was one of the stars of 2002 World Cup, where he terrorised defences.

DENIS IRWIN

Keano wasn't the only Corkman in the all-conquering Man Utd team of the 1990s. Mr Reliable, Denis Irwin, was the first name on the team sheet, Alex Ferguson often said. He won everything in the game and scored his fair share of goals – some from penalties and free kicks – even though he was a proper defender.

PACKIE BONNER

Bonner made the most famous save in Irish sports history. The Donegal man and Celtic keeper stopped a penalty kick from Romania's Daniel Timofte at Italia '90, helping Ireland to the World Cup quarter-finals. His long kicks, as he gritted his teeth, were an effective weapon for Jack Charlton. Bonnar learned to strike it so far by playing Gaelic football and practising with his twin brother, Denis, in a field near their home in Burtonport.

GEORGE BEST

One of football's first true superstars, the Belfast man helped Man Utd win the European Cup and won the European Player of the Year in 1968. He battled personal problems and didn't stay at the top of the game for as long as he could have but he's remembered still for his amazing skills. There's a statue outside Old Trafford of Georgie, with teammates Denis Law and Bobby Charlton.

KATIE McCABE

The brilliant women's national team qualified for the 2023 World Cup finals in Australia, and were led by skipper Katie McCabe, an all-action Dubliner who plays in midfield, while also playing wing back for Arsenal. She comes from a football-mad family of 11 kids – that's enough to field a team. Nowadays she plays Champions League football for one of the best sides in the world. She's also a proud supporter of LGBTQ+ rights.

IRISH WOMEN'S FOOTBALL

We all know girls can play football – and any sport – just well as boys. But sadly not everyone has believed that in the past. Despite the game being so popular, women's football was actually banned by the FA in 1921 – a rule that lasted over 50 years.

In Ireland, some of the first organised women's soccer teams were established in the 1970s. The first competitive game, between Ireland and Wales, took place in 1973 with the Irish winning away from home. For years the teams and leagues were under-supported and struggled, despite the commitment of excellent players and volunteers who believed in the game.

QUALIFYING

After years of near misses and heartbreak, Ireland's women qualified for the biggest tournament of all – a World Cup! – in 2022. Their journey to qualification wasn't easy though.

In 2019, a very experienced Dutch coach, Vera Pauw, took over the team. She promised to help the Girls in Green to fulfil their potential. After lots of hard work, Ireland got to a play-off with Scotland, Amber Barrett scoring the brilliant winner. The Girls in Green were drawn in what was seen as a group of death, with Canada and hosts Australia. They played valiantly in every match, and ended the pool with one point after a draw against Nigeria.

FIGHT FOR RESPECT

The women's national team are treated equally by the people who run Irish football now … but the team had to fight for that respect.

In 2017, the squad refused to go on a training camp before a game. Instead they told everyone – and the FAI – that they wanted to be treated a lot better. The players weren't being paid properly for missing work, they didn't have gym memberships and they sometimes had to change out of Ireland tracksuits in airport hotels and give them back! The men's team didn't have to do any of that.

In the end, the FAI came to an agreement with the players, who stood strong. Now, they are paid the same as the men's team and have much better conditions. That was the moment of change, and since they took that stand they've had great success on the international stage.

FUN FACT

The 2023 Women's World Cup had a full field of 32 teams for the first time, which meant countries like Ireland, Zambia and the Philippines could make their debuts at the tournament.

STEPHANIE ROCHE PUSKÁS GOAL

Stephanie Roche has played in the US, France and England as well as starring for Ireland over 50 times. In a 2018 game for Peamount United, Roche was playing a game against rivals Wexford Youths. She had two lovely touches of the ball when it came to her on the edge of the box. Her third touch was a wicked shot that flew into the Wexford Youths net.

It was such an incredible goal that it earned Roche a Puskás Award nomination. The award is given out for the best goal scored that year anywhere in the world – but it has to be filmed, you can't just tell them how good your goal was. Trust me…

ANNE O'BRIEN `TRAILBLAZER`

If women's football is at last getting the recognition it deserves, trailblazers like Anne O'Brien played a huge part in getting it there. O'Brien was born in Dublin in 1956, and grew up in Inchicore, where her talent became obvious to everyone at an early age.

When she was spotted playing for a team of the best Irish players called the All Stars, she signed for French club Stade de Reims. At just 17, she was the first Irish or British woman to become a professional player.

O'Brien won three league titles in France before moving to Rome to play for Lazio where she won six more league titles. She died in 2016 and is now remembered as one of the best players the country has ever produced.

EMMA BYRNE

When Ireland's women's footballers demanded the respect they deserved, Emma Byrne was front and centre as one of the squad's leaders. The Kildare native won 134 caps for her country and was a European and league champion with Arsenal. How'd she get so good? As a child, Byrne recalls her two elder brothers making her stand in goal as they pretended to be their football heroes. It wasn't long before they couldn't score past their sister.

DENISE O'SULLIVAN

Denise O'Sullivan is a street footballer at the centre of Ireland's midfield. The Cork woman was told she was too small to make it, but proved everyone wrong by becoming one of our most important players. Though she found it hard to leave her family in Knocknaheeny on the city's northside, she's travelled the world playing football with the best.

SOCCER AT HOME AND THE LEAGUE OF IRELAND

We're lucky to have our own leagues in this country with historic clubs, intense rivalries and amazing football. Some might say they're the greatest leagues in the world!

The League of Ireland is the competition that clubs in the Republic of Ireland play in.

There are 10 teams in the Premier Division and another 10 in the First Division. Shamrock Rovers are the most successful club with 20 league titles and counting.

The Women's National League started in 2011 and is growing every season – teams like Wexford Youths, Shelbourne and Peamount United have won lots of titles. Men's and women's sides also compete in the FAI Cup and get to play at Lansdowne Road if they make the final.

Derry City have played in the League of Ireland since the mid-1980s and have been very successful, but most teams in Northern Ireland play in the Irish League. Got it?

THE LEAGUE OF IRELAND

The League of Ireland was founded in 1921, and in its first season featured eight teams including Bohemians, Shelbourne and St James's Gate.

Dublin has clubs like Shamrock Rovers, Bohs, UCD, Shels and St Patrick's Athletic. Cork City was founded in 1984 after several Leeside clubs came and went. There are strong football traditions in towns and cities like Derry, Limerick, Waterford, Sligo, Longford and Athlone, who have all had success throughout the years with their proud clubs.

Games are typically played on Friday nights between February and October… just follow the floodlights and the smell of the chippy vans to your nearest ground.

BEST PLAYERS TO PLAY IN THE LEAGUE OF IRELAND

SEAMUS COLEMAN

Before Seamus Coleman was an Everton club legend and Ireland's captain, he was a great full back for Sligo Rovers. The Premier League club bought the Donegal man from the 'Bit o'Red' for just £60,000. What a bargain!

ROY KEANE

Cobh Ramblers played an important part in Roy Keane's development. He played in the Rams midfield before moving to Nottingham Forest. He's often seen back at St Colman's Park.

JACK BYRNE

Jack Byrne plays for Shamrock Rovers and is one of the most creative playmakers around. He returned from a stint in England at Man City and other clubs, and has also played in Cyprus.

PAUL MCGRATH

McGrath started his career with St Patrick's Athletic before signing for Manchester United in 1982 and Aston Villa in 1989. He was a key player for the Republic of Ireland national team and is considered one of the greatest defenders of all time.

KEVIN DOYLE

Wexford forward Kevin Doyle started his career with St Patrick's Athletic and then Cork City before moving to Reading, where he scored 55 goals in 164 appearances. He also played for Wolverhampton Wanderers and the national team.

JOEY N'DO

Joey N'Do was one of the best midfielders in the league during his time with Shels and Sligo Rovers. He was so good he was in the Cameroon squad at the 2002 World Cup.

Map locations

- DERRY CITY
- FINN HARPS
- SLIGO ROVERS
- LONGFORD TOWN
- DUNDALK
- DROGHEDA UTD.
- DLR WAVES FC
- BOHEMIANS
- PEAMOUNT UTD.
- SHELBOURNE
- ST PAT'S ATHLETICS
- UCD AFC
- SHAMROCK ROVERS
- GALWAY UTD.
- ATHLONE TOWN
- TREATY UTD.
- BRAY WANDERERS
- WEXFORD FC
- WEXFORD YOUTHS WFC
- KERRY FC
- WATERFORD
- COBH RAMBLERS
- CORK CITY

BEST EUROPEAN DISPLAYS

Irish clubs are often the underdogs in big European ties, but they've pulled off some memorable results over the years.

CORK CITY V BAYERN MUNICH, 1991
The German giants were 1-0 down to the Rebels thanks to a goal from Dave Barry, who won two All-Irelands with Cork's footballers. Bayern eventually got through, after a tough fight.

ATHLONE TOWN V AC MILAN, 1975
The Italian aristocrats tip-toed off their bus onto a muddy St Mel's Park for a game they drew nil-all. 'In Ireland today, there was a team of postmen, butchers and bakers that drew 0-0 with the mighty AC Milan,' the BBC News explained.

DUNDALK IN 2016
Stephen Kenny's Lilywhites Dundalk FC reached the group stages of the Europa League in the 2016–17 season. They were drawn against AZ Alkmaar, Maccabi Tel Aviv, and Zenit Saint Petersburg, and finished third in the group.

SHELS ON THE BRINK OF GLORY
Shelbourne reached the final qualifying round of the Champions League in 2004 where they faced the La Liga heavyweights Deportivo La Coruña. If they won they were into the group stages of Europe's top club competition. The Tolka Park side drew at home but eventually went down 3-0 in Spain.

MASCOTS

The League of Ireland mascots sometimes have a race to see who's the quickest. Some of the most beloved mascots from the league are:

1. Hooperman — (Shamrock Rovers)
2. Corky the Cheetah — (Cork City)
3. Paddy the Panther — (St Pat's)
4. Rocky the Seagull — (Bray Wanderers)
5. Leo the Lion — (Limerick)

19

A HISTORY OF THE GAA

Ireland's Gaelic games are made up of hurling, football, camogie, handball and rounders.

Hurling is one of the oldest field games in the world and has been played here, in some form, for at least 3,000 years! The ancient Celts played sports that were similar to our modern Gaelic games.

Hurling is mentioned in Irish legends like the story of Cú Chulainn, who earned his name after killing a fierce guard dog by driving a hurling ball – or sliothar – down his throat. The game was outlawed in the 12th century by the Normans, but it survived in various forms. By the middle of the 19th century, however, hurling was not widely popular.

DID YOU KNOW?

Irish people have spread their love of Gaelic games around the world and there are clubs in every place you can imagine from Sydney to Uganda to Cambodia.

London and New York have very strong GAA traditions and compete in the All-Ireland football championship.

FOUNDING OF THE GAA

The Gaelic Athletic Association was established in 1884 at a meeting in Hayes Hotel in Thurles, Co. Tipperary. The association was formed to revive Irish games and to encourage Irish people to play and support Gaelic sports. Though the games had been played for a long time, the GAA wanted to set rules and promote new clubs (as well as stop the spread of popular 'British' sports like soccer, rugby and cricket.)

The GAA's efforts were met with resistance from the British government, which saw the games as a way to promote Irish nationalism. Michael Davin became the association's first president and Michael Cusack was its secretary – if you go to a big match today in Croke Park, you might even sit in the Cusack or Davin Stand.

SAM MAGUIRE AND LIAM MACCARTHY

Two of the most famous trophies in Ireland are awarded to the winners of the hurling and football championships.

The Sam Maguire Cup is given to the winners of the All-Ireland senior football championship. The famous chalice is named after Sam Maguire from Dunmanway in West Cork, who was a prominent figure in the early years of the GAA and also involved in the Irish republican movement.

If you keep practising your swing, some day you might get the chance to lift the Liam MacCarthy Cup, the trophy awarded to the All-Ireland hurling champions. MacCarthy was born in London to Irish parents and was an active member of the association in the city and a member of the Irish Republican Brotherhood.

WOMEN'S GAMES

Ladies football and camogie are played in every parish in the country now. But the sports had to fight for recognition, and still do today, though the games are widely popular and highly skilled. The Ladies Football Association was formed in 1974 – in Hayes Hotel in Thurles. The Camogie Association had been set up much earlier, in 1904. The associations are technically separate to the GAA but clubs around the country share facilities and cooperate – and the organisations are expected to work even more closely together, or even merge, in the near future.

MÁIRE NÍ CHINNÉIDE

Máire Ní Chinnéide was passionate about the Irish language and culture – she was a playwright, activist, and sportswoman. During the Gaelic Revival, when our culture was going through a resurgence, she demanded camogie be part of the trend. She was part of the group of women who set up the Camogie Association, becoming its first president. She then scored the first ever goal in a competitive game in 1904. Beat that.

TRAILBLAZER

FIRST CHAMPIONSHIPS

The first All-Ireland championships were played in 1887 in hurling and football. In the first year, only 12 of our 32 counties were represented. Tipperary can claim to be the first hurling champions – they beat Galway in the final. Limerick overcame Louth in the football decider. The finals were held in different venues initially, but the 1895 finals were held at Jones, Road in Drumcondra. The GAA later bought the site and developed Croke Park.

HURLING AND CAMOGIE

CHRISTY RING

Christy Ring was a hurling icon and one of the best players to ever play the game. He was born just outside Cloyne, Co. Cork in 1920. He won his first proper hurley for having the best grades in his class, and was always seen practising with it and playing with his friends. Ring established himself as part of the Cork senior team and became known for his exceptional skill, toughness, accuracy and ability to perform under pressure. He became a star name after the classic Munster final replay of 1944 when his last-minute goal earned victory for Cork over Limerick.

Ring ultimately won eight All-Ireland senior hurling medals and nine Munster titles as well as starring for his club Glen Rovers in Cork city. He is the only player to line out for a county across four decades, playing his last game for Cork in 1964. He remained involved with successful Cork teams as a selector before he died suddenly in 1979 at just 58 years of age. At his huge funeral, his old teammate, Taoiseach Jack Lynch, made a famous graveside speech. 'Men who are fathers and grandfathers now will tell their children and grandchildren with pride that they saw Christy Ring play. The story will pass from generation to generation and so it will live.'

MOST SUCCESSFUL COUNTIES – CAMOGIE

1. Cork	29
2. Dublin	26
3. Kilkenny	14
4. Wexford	7
5. Antrim	6

CAMOGIE

Camogie is, of course, the version of hurling played by girls and women. At the start, teams consisted of 12 players but now it's 15-a-side. The first clubs were formed around 20 years after the founding of the GAA, and Louth and Dublin played the first All-Ireland final in 1912. These days our top intercounty players compete for the O'Duffy Cup which was named after Sean O'Duffy, a Mayo man who fought in the 1916 Rising and was later imprisoned. He also loved camogie and supported its development.

MOST SUCCESSFUL COUNTIES – HURLING

1. Kilkenny	36
2. Cork	30
3. Tipperary	28
4. Limerick	12
5. Dublin	6

THE THUNDER AND LIGHTNING FINAL

The All-Ireland hurling final of 1939 is famous for being a memorable contest between two rival teams, and the fact that it was played in crazy conditions.

Many supporters at Croke Park couldn't make out the identities of the players on the Cork and Kilkenny teams as they battled in a violent storm. It was so wet that the dye in the players' jerseys began to run! The future taoiseach Jack Lynch was the standout man for the Rebels but a late goal and free for the Cats saw them win what became known as the Thunder and Lightning Final.

FUN FACT

We've always known that hurling is one of the fastest field games in the world. But now we have the technology to measure it. T.J. Reid was clocked by Hawkeye technology striking a ball at Croke Park at an amazing 181 km/h.

WHAT'S IN A NAME?

Is it a hurley or a hurl? It's the debate that divides the country. In Munster, a hurling stick is mainly known as a hurley, while in the rest of the country you'll find people call it a hurl. And both camps think they're right. In a 2020 vote, 52% went with hurl.

CELTIC CROSSES

Winners of senior All-Ireland finals are awarded medals called Celtic Crosses. They are made of gold and show the logo of the GAA. A small replica of the Liam MacCarthy Cup is also awarded to the captain of the winning team.

THE SLIOTHAR

Keep your eye on the ball. The sliothar is the ball in the game of hurling and camogie. It was, at times, made up of materials like wood and animal hair, and in the old Brehon laws, it was said that compensation would be available for someone killed by a hurling ball. The modern sliothar was created in the early 20th century by Johnny McAuliffe and it's more or less the same now – a centre of cork, wrapped tightly in yarn and covered in two pieces of leather.

THE HURL/HURLEY

Hurling has been around a long time and the hurl – or hurley – has evolved in that time. As it's changed, even different parts of the country have variations on the hurling stick. It's traditionally made of ash wood, has a heel at the top to help with grip and a flattened bas – pronounced boss – at the other end, which is designed to strike or carry the ball. You might see a band tacked onto the bas to reinforce the stick. In Brehon laws only the king's son was allowed a bronze brace, while everyone else had to make do with copper.

GAELIC FOOTBALL

Gaelic football is one of the most popular games in Ireland and has been with us a long time. In fact, versions of the game existed through the Middle Ages. The game grew in the early 19th century with a cross-country version of the sport, called 'caid', which was very popular. Because of the impact of the famine, government opposition to Gaelic games, and increasing popularity of sports like cricket, Gaelic football became less popular. Interest in the game had shrunk until the foundation of the GAA. Since then Gaelic football has evolved and grown into the modern sport we love today.

DID YOU KNOW?
WRESTLING
It was an old GAA custom that players would wrestle with their direct opponents at the end of football or hurling matches to finish the day's action. But a rule was introduced in 1886 which banned this practice after complaints that the game was getting out of control.

BLOODY SUNDAY

On the morning of 21 November 1920, during the War of Independence, British forces opened fire on the crowd attending a Gaelic football match at Croke Park. Fourteen people were killed and dozens more were injured. Earlier that morning the Irish military unit called 'The Squad' killed 14 people and wounded others in a series of attacks across Dublin. Their aim was to assassinate British agents or spies. The British forces reacted brutally. Of those killed at the game between Tipperary and Dublin were three schoolboys aged 10, 11 and 14, a bride-to-be who was due to get married within days, as well as the Tipperary player Michael Hogan. The Hogan Stand is named after him today.

MICK O'DWYER   TRAILBLAZER

'Micko' is one of the most influential figures in the GAA's history. The Kerryman was involved in 21 senior All-Ireland football finals and won more than half of them. As a stylish player, he won four Celtic Crosses but made an even bigger impact when he took over the Kingdom as manager. Over 15 years the Waterville man led Kerry to 10 finals, winning eight of them, during a period of intense rivalry with Dublin.

> **DID YOU KNOW?**
> There are over 2,200 GAA clubs in Ireland.

POLO GROUNDS FINAL

The All-Ireland final of 1947 remains the only decider played outside of Ireland. Cavan were victorious against Kerry in New York's Polo Grounds, the home of the New York Giants baseball team at the time.

ARTANE BAND

Before every All-Ireland final, the Artane Band leads the players in a traditional parade around the pitch in front of the crowd. It's one of our most treasured sporting traditions. The band was founded in 1872 in what was then the Artane Industrial School for orphaned and abandoned boys. Now the band is made of boys and girls from throughout the community and they're a big part of our sporting heritage.

> **DID YOU KNOW?**
> **THE INVENTION OF THE SOLO**
> One of the most exciting sights in Gaelic football is seeing a player hare down the pitch soloing the ball. Sean Lavin, who was born in Mayo in 1898, is said to have invented the solo run in a game with Dublin in 1921. He scored a point at the end of the run but the confused referee disallowed it. One of the most important skills of the game was born however.

THE DOUBLE

Lots of us have been lucky enough to have seen our county win a hurling or football championship. But Cork are the only county to win the Liam MacCarthy Cup and Sam Maguire in the same season. In 1990, the Rebels' hurlers won a thrilling final against Galway and two weeks later Billy Morgan's footballers sealed the achievement with a narrow win over their archrivals Meath. Teddy McCarthy played on both teams and won two All-Irelands in two weeks, the only player ever to do it.

THE MAYO CURSE

The curse, they say, began as Mayo celebrated All-Ireland victory in 1951. The county had beaten Meath in Croke Park and the players returned with the Sam Maguire. One version of the myth suggests the players failed to pay their respects to a passing funeral as they rolled through Foxford. An angry priest hissed: 'For as long as you all live, Mayo won't win another All-Ireland.' He turned out to be right, but was it because of a curse? Clare hurlers also suffered an apparent 'curse', waiting 81 years to win their second All-Ireland in 1995.

OUR OTHER GAMES

Hurling, camogie and football may be what come to mind first when you think about Gaelic games. But the GAA is about more than just those great sports. We love to play handball, rounders and athletics and our players have made an impact far from Ireland in different codes.

POC FADA

The annual Poc Fada competition takes place in the Cooley Peninsula in Co. Louth. The competition tries to find the player with the longest strike of a sliotar. The contest has its beginnings in the legend of the Táin, where the tale of Setanta driving his sliotar into Emain Macha is told. Goalkeepers like Ger Cunningham from Cork and Tipperary's Brendan Cummins have dominated the competition over the years.

THE DEVELOPMENT OF THE MODERN HURLEY DESIGN

Hurleys are traditionally made of ash wood – though bamboo is becoming more popular. The strong base of the ash tree is best for hurleys. Hurley makers use old production techniques and make sticks by hand with their tools. People often come from far away to buy a stick from a renowned hurley maker. Often the skill is passed down from generation to generation.

SHINTY

Ireland and Scotland share a Gaelic heritage that is reflected in the game of hurling and the Scots' sport shinty. Shinty, which is traditionally played in the Scottish Highlands, is similar to hurling. But there are lots of differences too. The shinty stick doesn't have a bas, the games are 90 minutes long and the goalkeeper – on a team of 12 – is the only player who's allowed to handle the ball. Every year a game is played between a team of hurlers from Ireland and a Scottish shinty side. The players can use their own style of stick and some of the rules are a compromise.

INTERNATIONAL RULES

International Rules or Compromise Rules is a mix of Gaelic football and Australian Rules football. It borrows rules from both games with some fixtures between Ireland and Australia played with a round ball and some with a rugby style ball. Sometimes the games are played on a rectangular pitch like GAA players are used to but sometimes they have to play in an oval. Players need to get used to big hits, with the Aussie Rules style tackle often allowed. Some of the games over the years have gotten very rough! The trophy awarded to the captain of the winning International Rules team was named after Cormac McAnallen, after the Tyrone skipper's tragic death in 2004.

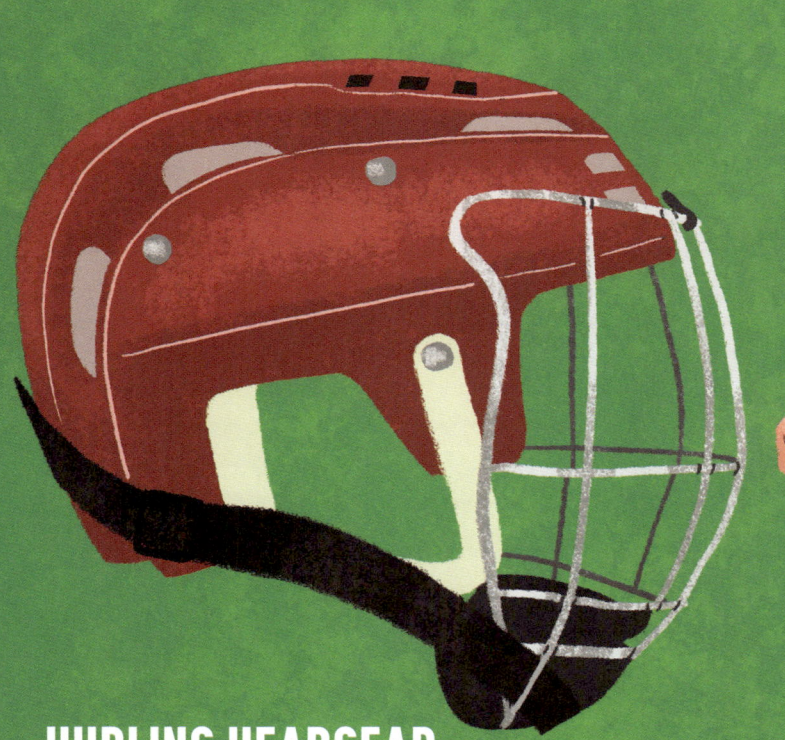

HURLING HEADGEAR

Everyone playing hurling has to wear proper headgear now, but that wasn't always the case. The GAA voted to make helmets with a face guard compulsory in 2008. The practice only came into being in the 1970s and hurlers were slow to strap on a full helmet.

HANDBALL

Handball is a fast, very skilful game where the aim is to strike (with your hand) the ball against a wall and make it bounce twice before your opponent gets to it. It's been played here for a long time, with the earliest record in Galway's town statutes in 1527, which forbade the playing of ball games against the town walls.

ROUNDERS

Rounders is a ball and bat game that you may have played in school. It's also one of the four official sports of the GAA. It might remind you of baseball and, in fact, it's thought 'America's pastime' came from our rounders sport in some way or another.

DOWN UNDER

Lots of Gaelic footballers have made the transition from our game to Australian Rules football, playing professionally in Aussie Rules 'footie'. In recent years, the likes of Dublin footballer Sinéad Goldrick and Zach Tuohy from Laois have won premiership medals with their clubs in Oz.

JIM STYNES

Born in Dublin in 1966, Stynes is arguably our most famous Australian Football League export and would go on to become one of the most iconic figures in Australian sporting history. In 1984 Stynes joined the Melbourne Football Club, making his debut in the AFL in 1987. He went on to become a club legend, winning the prestigious Brownlow medal for the league's best player.

He became the Demons' longest-serving captain, played a record 244 consecutive games, won four Best and Fairest awards, and earned All-Australian honours. Off the field, his impact extended far beyond his athletic achievements and for his charity work he was awarded the Medal of the Order of Australia (OAM) in 2007. Stynes died after a long battle with cancer in 2012 but his legacy lives on today.

THE GREATEST HURLING AND CAMOGIE PLAYERS OF ALL TIME

KATHLEEN MILLS-HILL

'Kay' Mills-Hill is regarded as camogie's first superstar. She played senior intercounty for Dublin for 20 years, making her debut in 1941 at 16 years of age, winning an incredible 15 All-Ireland camogie medals. It's a record that is likely never to be matched. The midfielder was small and skilful and known for her long-range lobbed goal. Every year the captain of the winning team in the All-Ireland Junior camogie final is presented with a trophy named after Mills-Hill.

BRIEGE CORKERY AND RENA BUCKLEY

Mills-Hill held the record for most total All-Ireland medals until she was overtaken by two dual players from Cork. Briege Corkery and Rena Buckley ended up with 18 medals. Each! They sometimes even had to play a game of hurling and football for their county in one day. Buckley captained Cork's footballers to glory in 2012 and decided to give her speech entirely in Irish. When she led the camogie team to success five years later, she did it again. Maith thú, Rena. She finished her career with a record 11 football titles and seven in camogie; Corkery later bowed out with the same incredible tally.

HENRY SHEFFLIN

If you earn the nickname 'The King', you know you've done okay. Brian Cody's Kilkenny team were the most successful ever, filled with all-time great players. They all looked to the Ballyhale forward, as their leader and he is regarded as one of the best players to ever grip a hurley. He won a record 10 All-Ireland championship titles with the Noresiders and loads more with his club. In fact, he is one of only a handful of people to win an All-Ireland with his club as a player and manager. He must have a big mantelpiece at home because he also won six National Hurling League titles, 13 Leinster championships and 11 All Stars awards.

JOHN DOYLE

The 'Holycross Hercules' earned mythical status for his glittering career with Tipperary. In the mid '60s he formed part of a formidable half-back line that became known as 'Hell's Kitchen'. Gulp. He often took on titans of the game like Christy Ring, and was the Premier County's talisman over a couple of decades. He capped his career by becoming the hurler of the year in 1964 and then by claiming a joint-record (at the time) eighth All-Ireland medal in 1965, drawing level with Ring.

BRIAN WHELAHAN

One of the most stylish hurlers we've seen, Brian Whelahan won it all including two All-Ireland titles with Offay, four All-Ireland medals with his club Birr, four All Stars awards and two Hurler of the Year awards. More importantly he was a huge part of one of the most beloved teams, who helped redefine hurling in the 1990s. And after all that he was named on the GAA's Hurling Team of the Millenium. We'll have to wait over 900 years to see who gets on the next one.

MICK MACKEY

Mackey won three All-Ireland titles with Limerick and it's thought that he passed the baton to Ring as the best player around when he called time on his career. The Ahane man helped the Treaty County dominate the game from 1933 to 1940. In 1988 the main covered stand in the Gaelic Grounds in Limerick was named the Mackey Stand in his honour.

SEANIE MCMAHON

When Clare ended their 81-year title famine in 1995 they had a team full of big talents and bigger personalities. Seanie McMahon was arguably the most important cog in Ger Loughnane's winning machine. Probably the finest centre-back of his generation, he is one of hurling's true all-time greats. He was clever, skilful and brave – he even played a championship match against Cork in 1995 with a broken collarbone!

ANGELA DOWNEY

Angela Downey is considered one of the greatest camogie players to play the game. Born in 1958 in Ballyragget, along with her twin sister Ann - who was also a very successful camogie player - she went on to become one of the most decorated players in the sport. During a brilliant career with Kilkenny between 1974 and 1996, she won 12 All-Ireland medals, 13 Leinster titles and was named on the Camogie Team of the Century.

JOE CANNING

Joe Canning was a prodigy, winning two All-Ireland minor championships and an under-21 title and people were screaming for him to step up to the senior Galway team. In his first year in the grade he won an All Star and a Young Hurler of the Year award. But it wasn't always easy; despite his great talent and effort, he could never quite help Galway to win the big one. Until 2017 … Canning cut one of his trademark sidelines over the bar to beat Tipp in a semi-final epic and Galway brought Liam west after a final win over Waterford. He retired in 2021 and is regarded as one of the best hurlers ever.

29

THE GREATEST GAELIC FOOTBALLERS OF ALL TIME

PÁIDÍ Ó SÉ

Páidí Ó Sé was a tough defender with Kerry, winner of eight All-Irelands on the pitch and the man who ended a long wait in the Kingdom for the Sam Maguire as manager. Ó Sé came from Ventry on the Dingle Peninsula, in the Irish-speaking gaeltacht of Kerry. He trained by running on the beach, across the dunes and along the country roads. A key part of Mick O'Dwyer's famous teams, Ó Sé had a huge, charismatic personality and his pub in Ceann Trá is famous throughout Ireland. After his playing days, he successfully managed Kerry, winning the All-Ireland in 1997, as well as bringing Westmeath to their first ever Leinster title in 2004 before managing Clare as well.

STEPHEN CLUXTON

The best Gaelic football goalkeeper of all time and one of the most influential players in the game's history, Cluxton kicked off an amazing era for Dublin by striking an incredible winning point in the All-Ireland final against Kerry in 2011.

He also changed the game of football, controlling the distribution of the ball from kickouts, and making plenty of saves too. He led the Dubs quietly and didn't like to do many interviews or give long speeches. In 2023, 'Clucko' came out of retirement to help lead Dublin to another All-Ireland win. Along with James McCarthy and Mick Fitzsimons, Cluxton now holds a record nine All-Ireland Senoir Football medals.

CORA STAUNTON

You can try to measure Cora Staunton's impact through stats. The Mayo woman is Ladies Football all-time top scorer – she scored 59 goals and 476 points! She won four All-Irelands with her county, six with her club and earned 11 All Stars awards. But her impact was bigger than those numbers. Staunton is regarded as the best women's footballer ever and helped change women's sport in Ireland. Though she excelled as a Gaelic footballer, Staunton is a multi-sport talent. She was the first international player to be recruited to the AFLW in Australia and blazed a trail in that game for Irishwomen too.

PETER CANAVAN

When he finally lifted the Sam Maguire in 2003, Peter Canavan also shed the tag of 'Greatest Footballer Never to Win an All-Ireland'. The Red Hand talisman was named Player of the Year in 1995, but lost the final to Dublin. When the county lost to Galway in 2001, many thought his chance had passed.

Tyrone boss Micky Harte guided the county to the decider in '03, however, and they finally won. Two years later, an ageing Canavan was substituted in another final, then reintroduced with seven minutes to go. The stadium went wild! Canavan, a teacher, linked up with former student Owen Mulligan for a memorable goal and Tyrone won another All-Ireland.

CIARÁN MCDONALD

Ciarán McDonald retired without the All-Ireland medal his talent deserved, but his flair and skill earned him the love of many sports fans. The Crossmolina man shone in the green and red of Mayo – as well as white boots and braids, at times. He was a star man for Ireland against Australia in International Rules series and lit up grounds at Croke Park and beyond.

SEÁN PURCELL

The Galway man is considered one of the finest players of the game ever and it's said he could play anywhere on the pitch. The Tuam man really shone at centre forward, however, and it's there he earned a place on the Team of the Century and the Team of the Millennium.

COLM COOPER

Sometimes a player is so good everyone comes to know them by their first name. Or in Colm Cooper's case, his nickname: The Gooch. Growing up in Kerry, Cooper was never the biggest or strongest player but he was very skilful and practised his shooting and passing a lot. He was soon playing for the Kingdom's senior side and ended a glittering career with five All-Ireland titles.

MICK O'CONNELL

When Mick O'Connell set off on his journey to Croke Park, he'd often have to row his own boat from his home on the isolated Valentia Island to the mainland in Kerry.

He made his senior debut for Kerry in 1956 and was soon considered one of the best players in the country. Admired for his graceful play and high leaps, he won four All-Ireland medals and 12 Munster medals.

Regarded as one of the most stylish footballers to play the game, he is still the yardstick for players today and was named on the Football Team of the Millenium and Century.

SUE RAMSBOTTOM

Sue Ramsbottom had to wait a long time for All-Ireland glory. She suffered seven final defeats before finally becoming a champion in 2001 with her county, Laois. Away from the pitch, she was training to be an army officer and even brought her two daughters for a tour of duty in Bosnia. As well as being the O'Moore county's taliswoman, Ramsbottom took up rugby and eventually played for Ireland.

☆ GOLDEN AGES ☆

GAELIC FOOTBALL

CORK LADIES FOOTBALL

Cork's ladies footballers had never, in their history, won a senior Munster or All-Ireland title before their breakthrough in 2004. From there they went on to win 10 of the next 11 All-Irelands. Under 'The Master' Eamonn Ryan, the so called Rebellettes battled to lots of close-fought title wins – they took those 10 Brendan Martin Cup victories, as well as 9 national league titles and 10 provincial victories.

How did they do it? A group of experienced, quality players like Juliet Murphy were helped by a talented crop of youngsters like Rena Buckley, Briege Corkery and Valerie Mulcahy, guided by a canny manager in Ryan. He helped the group achieve their potential. The Cork LGFA team defined an era and certainly reached new heights for their county and their game.

DUBLIN'S SIX IN A ROW

The 'six in a row' of All-Ireland football titles is the greatest team achievement in men's Gaelic games. Dublin has a rich tradition in Gaelic football going back to 'Heffo's Army' and their battles with Kerry in the 1970s and 80s. But they had underachieved for many years – apart from a single season of success in 1995.

The Dubs finally made the breakthrough in 2011 under Pat Gilroy, kicking off a decade of glory. Jim Gavin took over as manager and the air force pilot plotted a course to an historic run of All-Irelands. He had many excellent players with him, like captain Stephen Cluxton, the sharpshooting Brogan brothers, the high-fielding Brian Fenton and tough defender Philly McMahon.

Mayo in particular pushed the Dubs close most years – almost besting them in finals in 2013, '16 and '17; but the Blues always won the day. The crowds on Hill 16 will always remember the incredible run from their team, the best Gaelic football side ever.

KERRY GOLD

The great Kerry team – and their rivalry with Dublin in the 1970s and 80s – helped create the modern game we love today. The Kingdom team, who played with style, won seven All-Ireland titles between 1978 and 1986. For a long time they were considered the best team to ever play the game.

They had star players like Pat Spillane, Jack O'Shea and Mikey Sheehy who had huge talent but worked as hard as anyone. Their old-school trainer Mick O'Dwyer once had them out training 27 nights in a row. Kerry are top of the Gaelic football roll of honour because of their rich football tradition. The team of the 70s and 80s added the most glorious chapter to their story.

☆ GOLDEN AGES ☆

HURLING

KILKENNY HURLING – THE CODY ERA

Brian Cody and his Kilkenny team brought the game of hurling to a new level with their ferocious and skilful play, which brought unprecedented success. Cody – a no-nonsense manager who liked to keep things simple – took over the Cats in 1998. He lost an All-Ireland final in his first year in charge to old rivals Cork, but after that setback he built a series of teams that dominated the game.

The Noresiders won 43 major honours under Cody – top of the list were 11 All-Irelands, including an historic four in a row between 2006 and 2009, with a team featuring greats like Henry Shefflin, Tommy Walsh and J.J. Delaney. Their achievements were enhanced by rivalries with first Cork and later Galway and Tipperary, who pushed the Cats on many thrilling occasions.

HURLING'S REVOLUTION YEARS

For many years, hurling was dominated by the 'traditional' powers of Cork, Kilkenny and Tipperary, who shared the Liam MacCarthy between them from year to year. But when the swashbuckling Offaly team arrived to win the All-Ireland in 1994 it sparked an exciting mid-90s period when several counties made historic breakthroughs.

Ger Loughnane's brilliant Clare team – with players including Jamesie O'Connor, 'Sparrow' O'Loughlin, P.J. 'Fingers' O'Connell and the superb Brian Lohan – ended their title famine in 1995 and won again in 1997. Offaly succeeded again, dramatically, in 1998 and Wexford ended their long wait for another title in 1996. This exciting period became known as the Revolution Years and changed the landscape of the sport forever.

CROKE PARK

Croke Park is not just a stadium where Gaelic games are played. It's a place that symbolises the evolution and strength of the GAA and our national games. It's also been the scene for historically important events, and has played a huge role in Irish life for over a century.

As well as showcasing our GAA greats, the stadium has also hosted major boxing matches, crucial soccer and rugby internationals, a Cowboy Skills Rodeo in 1924 and major music events by the likes of U2, Westlife and Taylor Swift.

The first Gaelic games were played on Jones' Road in the 1880s when the site was known as the City And Suburban Sports Grounds. The site was then purchased by former GAA President Frank Dineen in 1908 for £3,250, who could see the site had great potential for the future of the GAA. The GAA bought the stadium in 1913 from Dineen for £3,500 and named it after their former patron Archbishop Croke, who had died in 1902.

During the War of Independence, the stadium was an important place for fundraisers and political gatherings. In November 1920, it was the site of what became known as Bloody Sunday, one of the worst atrocities of the war and an important turning point in the military struggle with Britain.

During that fateful game between Dublin and Tipperary, British forces killed 14 civilians including Premier County player Michael Hogan. The Hogan Stand was later built and named in the player's honour in 1926.

The first scoreboard was installed in 1925 and something we're so used to – the playing of the national anthem before a game – took place for the first time a year later.

The Association continued to invest in the ground as our national games grew in popularity, and the Cusack Stand was opened in 1938. The following season, hurling fans were able to sit in the grandstand's new benches to witness the now famous Thunder and Lightning Final.

The Canal End and Nally End terraces opened in the early 1950s and a record 84,856 spectators watched Cork and Wexford contest the 1954 hurling final. The record for a football final is 90,556 – with Down and Offaly in 1961 drawing the biggest crowd.

The stadium continued to improve and change the way it looked until an almost complete redevelopment was undertaken in the 1990s. A museum was added, the famous stands were rebuilt and modern facilities added. It's now one of the biggest and best stadiums in the world with a long and eventful history.

THE AVIVA

The Aviva Stadium may look very modern and new but the stadium at Lansdowne Road has a history stretching back over 150 years. During that time, it has been the home of our soccer and rugby teams, as well as the fans' 'Lansdowne Roar'.

The sportsman Henry Wallace Dunlop founded Lansdowne Road Stadium in 1872 as the first international sporting venue in the world. The ground was named in honour of the third Marquess of Lansdowne, and was first a multi-purpose sports complex for the Irish Champion Athletic Club.

You might imagine a football or rugby pitch when you think of the stadium but initially there was a running track, a tennis club, a croquet green, an archery facility *and* some pitches.

The first athletics international took place at the Dublin 4 venue when Ireland met England in 1875 and many running stars like Ronnie Delany featured there over the years.

In 1876, Lansdowne Road witnessed the first interprovincial rugby game here with Leinster and Ulster facing off for the first time. They'd contest a European Cup final at the Aviva Stadium 136 years later. In 1878, the Irish Rugby Football Union hosted England at the stadium in the first international there, with the visitors winning .

The IRFU set about improving the stadium once they gained full ownership in the early 1900s. The pitch was turned around to face another way and the West Stand was covered.

As well as witnessing many Five Nations games and Tests with southern hemisphere sides throughout the century, the stadium became the home of Irish football. Jack Charlton's side made it a fortress and had many happy afternoons and nights there. It was also the scene of a riot by visiting English fans in 1995, which saw the friendly game against Charlton's home country abandoned. Ireland were 1-0 up at the time thanks to a David Kelly goal.

The old stadium was knocked down and rebuilt in the 2000s. At the time it was the oldest international stadium in Europe and the oldest rugby ground in the world. The new stadium was designed to squeeze in next to the neighbouring houses and the DART line which provides the familiar sound of a train chugging by during games. The new stadium looks a lot different but the walk to the familiar spot is the same for soccer and rugby fans.

As well as sporting contests, huge stars like Rihanna and Harry Styles have filled the seats of the stadium, and other sports like American Football and lacrosse have showcased their games there too.

A HISTORY OF RUGBY IN IRELAND

Legend has it that rugby was invented when William Webb Ellis, a pupil at the posh Rugby School in England in the 1820s, picked up the ball during a football match and ran with it. By the end of the century, it was a global game.

Rugby spread around the world thanks to British soldiers, sailors and others and grew to be especially popular in Ireland, South Africa, France, Australia and New Zealand.

Played by amateurs for many years, rugby turned professional in 1995. The Webb Ellis trophy is now awarded to winners of the World Cup every four years.

In Ireland, the game has been played since at least 1854, when the first club was founded in Trinity College Dublin. The Irish Rugby Football Union (IRFU), which still runs the game here today, was formed in 1874.

The first Ireland international game was a 20-a-side game against England in February 1875. Four years later, Ireland lined out in a 15-a-side tie.

The game grew in popularity and clubs were formed all around the country. By the time the All Blacks visited Dublin for the first time in November 1905, the IRFU had to make the game an all-ticket event due to high demand. New Zealand set the tone for the next century by winning 15-0.

THE GAME OF RUGBY

One of the most physically demanding and technical games, rugby is played by two teams of 15 on a 100-metre-long pitch with an oval ball, to make things even more interesting.

SCHOOLS

Ireland has four professional teams in Munster, Leinster, Ulster and Connacht and many clubs. The top clubs compete in the All-Ireland League. As well as that, some schools are very important to the development of the game in Ireland. In Leinster, the best rugby-playing sides face off in the Leinster Senior Cup, with Blackrock the top side. Teams from Cork and Limerick are the traditional powerhouses in the Munster Senior Cup. Most of our international players have come through this competitive schools system.

POSITIONS

A rugby team consists of eight forwards and seven backs. The forwards are made up of the big guys in the front row – two props and a hooker – and even *bigger* guys in the second row called locks. Then there's an athletic back row of two flankers and a number eight.

In the backs, the important scrum half is often the smallest player on the pitch. Tenacious and skilful, he follows and distributes the ball. The fly-half or out-half wears No. 10 and is the team's general – he moves the team up the pitch and usually kicks the ball most. The two centres in the midfield are important in defence and attack, while the wingers and full back are the last line of defence but are important in finishing tries or breaking the defensive lines too.

POSITIONS BY NUMBERS

1 LOOSEHEAD PROP
2 HOOKER
3 TIGHTHEAD PROP
4 LEFT LOCK
5 RIGHT LOCK
6 BLINDSIDE FLANKER
7 OPENSIDE FLANKER
8 NUMBER EIGHT, DUH
9 SCRUM HALF
10 FLY-HALF OR OUT-HALF
12 INSIDE CENTRE
11 LEFT WING
13 OUTSIDE CENTRE
14 RIGHT WING
15 FULL BACK

DAVE GALLAHER

David Gallaher was born in Ramleton in Co. Donegal in 1873. His family emigrated when he was a child as part of a scheme to settle people in New Zealand. Gallaher had to leave school early after his mother died and his father struggled to find work, but he was very good at sports like cricket and rugby. His promising rugby career stalled when he enlisted in the army and went to fight in the Boer War, where he won medals for his bravery.

When his rugby career resumed he earned a call-up to the New Zealand national team. He was chosen as the captain of the team now known as the Original All Blacks of 1905–06. The team were the first New Zealand squad to tour Britain and Ireland. Under Gallaher they only ever lost one game and they impressed with skilful and physical performances. The team did a lot to establish the legend of the All Blacks jersey and they're revered in the country still.

Gallaher wrote a book with his co-captain on how to play the game and was a successful coach after his retirement. When World War I broke out he enlisted in the army again and was killed in the Battle of Passchendaele in Belgium in 1917, aged 43. The boy from Donegal is remembered as a brilliant leader and a key part of the All Blacks story. He was inducted into the World Rugby Hall of Fame, and France and New Zealand play for the Dave Gallaher Trophy.

THE FOUR PROVINCES

CONNACHT

STADIUM: The Sportsground, Galway
COLOUR: Green

Often the underdogs of Irish rugby, Connacht have a long and proud tradition. The branch was formed when six clubs from the province met in 1885 with the aim of promoting the game in the west. Henry J. Anderson was the first Connacht player to line out for Ireland, and later, when president of the club, he opened the Sportsground in Galway, where they still play today.

In 2003, the province faced extinction. There were plans to disband the club to save money. Rugby supporters from the west protested on the streets and made their love of Connacht Rugby clear. The club survived, and in 2016 pulled off a stunning league victory in the PRO12 under manager Pat Lam. Connacht regularly play top-level European rugby and provide players to Ireland's national team.

DID YOU KNOW?
Connacht fans sing 'The Fields of Athenry' all over Europe as they support their team.

STAR PLAYER: BUNDEE AKI

Of Samoan heritage, Bundee Aki was born and raised in New Zealand, but has made his home in Galway. He's been the centre of Connacht's success since arriving in 2014 and has won dozens of Ireland caps at centre.

LEINSTER

STADIUM: The RDS/Aviva Stadium, Dublin
COLOURS: Blue

For a long time in the professional era, Leinster struggled to break through, but now they are the most successful province in Ireland. The Blues won their first European title in 2009, thanks to players like Brian O'Driscoll, Gordon D'Arcy and Johnny Sexton. They've gone on to add three more stars to their jersey, making them one of the heavyweights of continental rugby.

DID YOU KNOW?
Leinster's European Cup clash against Munster at Croke Park in 2009 set a world record for a club rugby game with a crowd of over 82,000.

MEMORABLE MATCH
The 2011 European Cup final looked over at half time. Northampton Saints had dominated Leinster in the game at a sold-out Millennium Stadium in Cardiff. The English side led 22-6 at the break. Johnny Sexton made a passionate speech in the dressing-room, telling his teammates the game wasn't over. The out-half personally scored 22 second-half points, his teammates held the Saints scoreless and Leinster won the European Cup by a scoreline of 33-22.

DID YOU KNOW?
Every time a rugby club wins the European Cup they get the famous trophy – but they earn something else too. Just like with your schoolwork, good effort gets a star. Clubs can stitch one star per win over their crest. Leinster have a constellation of four stars.

STAR PLAYER: ROCKY ELSOM

Leinster had lots of Irish talent in their squad but constantly fell short of winning the big prizes. There was something missing. Rocky Elsom brought the aggression that they needed in 2008 and helped them win their first European title.

MUNSTER

STADIUM: Thomond Park, Limerick/Musgrave Park, Cork
COLOURS: Red

Munster's fans sing 'Stand Up and Fight', a song that sums up how the southern province plays. Munster has a long tradition of playing hard and winning despite being up against it sometimes. The province is made up of clubs with proud histories, especially in Limerick, Tipperary and Cork. Since the professional era began, Munster have given us some of Irish rugby's most memorable games, particularly in the first decade of the twenty-first century, when they won two European Cups in '06 and '08.

ALL BLACKS IN 1978

Books and plays have been written about Munster's win over the mighty All Blacks at Thomond Park, probably the most legendary game in Irish rugby. Ireland had never beaten the New Zealand national team until recent years so for the province to pull it off was incredible.

GREAT PLAYER : JOHN HAYES

John Hayes didn't start playing rugby until he was 18, when he went along to Bruff rugby club in Limerick with some friends. Known as 'The Bull', the big and strong farmer went on to win everything with Munster and played over 200 times for the province at prop.

ULSTER

STADIUM: Ravenhill, currently known as Kingspan Stadium, Belfast
COLOURS: White

Fans regularly fill the 18,000-capacity Belfast stadium to produce the 'Ravenhill roar' in support of Ulster. During the amateur era, Ulster were very successful and in the 1980s and '90s were the dominant province, winning 10 Interpro titles in a row.

EUROPEAN GLORY

After professionalism, Ulster became the first Irish team to win the European Cup in 1999. The northern province beat Colomiers 21-6 at Lansdowne in 1999.

DID YOU KNOW?

Ulster Rugby's crest features a red hand with two rugby balls – the red hand comes from the province's coat of arms, which has origins in ancient Gaelic Ireland.

GREAT PLAYER: DAVID HUMPHREYS

A hometown hero, Humphreys was Ulster's leader in two periods with the province. As skipper and No. 10, he won the Heineken Cup as well as clinching the Celtic League for the club with a last-minute kick. When he retired – a club legend – he was Ulster's most capped player and the league's top scorer. He went on to serve the club as director of rugby.

IRISH INTERNATIONAL RUGBY

THE SIX NATIONS

OLD RIVALS

Ireland competes in the Six Nations championship every spring with northern hemisphere rivals England, France, Italy, Scotland and Wales. The team with the most points wins the championship of course but there are various other trophies and titles up for grabs.

ENDING THE LONG WAIT

Ireland had to wait 61 years for a Grand Slam. In 2009, Declan Kidney's side had to beat Wales in Cardiff to achieve a clean sweep – but the hosts were playing for a title too.

It looked like Irish fans would be celebrating when Ronan O'Gara dropped a goal late on to put his side ahead. Under huge pressure he kept his head down and split the posts with his kick. But there was time for more drama when Wales were awarded a penalty. The usually reliable Stephen Jones tried to claim the title for his side with the last kick of the championship, but it came up just short. The win sealed a first championship since 1985, first Grand Slam since 1948 and kickstarted an amazing period in Irish rugby.

GRAND SLAM: Achieved by winning all your games.

THE CENTENARY QUAICH: The cup that Ireland and Scotland battle for when they meet.

CALCUTTA CUP: The old trophy that England and Scotland play for each year.

TRIPLE CROWN: Can be won by Ireland, Scotland, Wales or England by beating all the other nations.

MILLENNIUM TROPHY: First awarded in 1988, this is awarded after each match between England and Ireland.

'IRELAND'S CALL'

Ireland's rugby team represents the entire island. Because 'Amhrán na BhFiann' is the Republic of Ireland's anthem and doesn't represent the tradition of some players and fans from the north of Ireland, a new song was commissioned for the Irish rugby team. The composer Phil Coulter wrote 'Ireland's Call' ahead of the 1995 World Cup and it's played before each international game now. 'Amhran na Bhfiann' is sung too when the Ireland team plays in Dublin.

DID YOU KNOW?

At the 1987 World Cup, organisers in New Zealand surprised the Ireland team by playing 'The Rose of Tralee' as our anthem.

THE WORLD CUP

For many years international teams competed in traditional and exciting competitions like the Six Nations in Europe or the Tri Nations Series in the southern hemisphere. But in 1987, rugby went global with the first World Cup. The tournament was held in New Zealand and Australia with 16 teams invited. The All Blacks beat the French in the final to claim the first title. The tournament is held every four years, and up to 2023, Ireland had never managed to get past the quarter-final stage in the men's game. Andy Farrell's side is the number 1 ranked team in the world heading into the 2023 World Cup in France, though – who knows what they might achieve!

RUGBY AT CROKE PARK

While Lansdowne Road stadium was being redeveloped, the GAA were asked if they'd change their rules and let rugby and soccer be played in Croke Park. GAA members voted in 2005 to suspend Rule 42, which prohibited the playing of non-Gaelic games at GAA grounds.

It was an historic decision – Croke Park would be able to host Six Nations rugby games. France came to Dublin during the 2007 Six Nations and lined out on the famous Jones, Road pitch. Les Bleus struck late and won the game. A few weeks later, England came to GAA HQ for an even more emotional and exciting occasion. Some people were worried about the British anthem playing at the site of Bloody Sunday (see page 24).

England's players and supporters were, of course, welcomed to the stadium, but when the game kicked off Ireland were determined to make up for the French loss.

When Shane Horgan scored a try by leaping high to collect a cross-field kick from Ronan O'Gara, it capped a resounding 43-13 win.

SOLDIER FIELD, CHICAGO

Ireland had never beaten the All Blacks in 111 years by the time the teams met in a special game in Chicago in 2016. Joe Schmidt's side were, by then, one of the best teams in the world and had almost made history against New Zealand three years earlier – this time they wouldn't let it slip. The former Ireland international and Munster rugby legend Anthony Foley had died in the weeks prior to the Soldier Field clash. As the All Blacks performed their haka, the 15 Irish players formed a figure of eight shape to face the challenge, in honour of Foley's jersey number.

Ireland wouldn't be beaten that day. They finished 40-29 winners on a special night for Irish rugby.

IRISH WOMEN'S RUGBY

Women's rugby in Ireland has come a long way thanks to the work of those who love the game and demanded better support for the players and coaches here.

The Women's Rugby Football Union was set up in Britain in 1983 and the first official women's Rugby World Cup was held in 1998 (with an unofficial tournament in 1991). Ireland were absent from both.

In 1992, a group of women met in the living room of Mary O'Beirne's house in Dublin. They were determined to push the women's game forward in Ireland. They formed the Ireland Women's Rugby Football Union (IWRFU), and O'Beirne was elected as its first president. They worked hard and promoted the women's game, which had to fight for coverage and support. An appearance at the 1998 World Cup in the Netherlands was a big milestone for Ireland.

In 2001, it was announced that the men's union, the IRFU, and the IWRFU would join together. It was great news. Four years later Ireland won their first Women's Six Nations game, and the foundations were there for Irish women's rugby to succeed.

THE FIRST GAME

Ireland's women played their first rugby international on 14 February – Valentine's Day – in 1993. Jill Henderson, our first captain, brought her team to play Scotland for what would be the hosts' first international. They played the game at Raeburn Place, where the first-ever men's rugby international took place in 1871. Scotland ran out 10-0 winners against Henderson's Ireland, but we were up and running.

GRAND SLAM AND BLACK FERNS

After years of struggling to earn recognition from the media and Irish sports fans, the teams of 2013 and 2014 at last got the attention they deserved. Thanks to the work of the barrier-breakers before them and their own success on the pitch, Ireland were in the spotlight. They kicked off a special period in Irish women's sport by beating Wales in Port Talbot in February 2013. Packed with strong characters like skipper Fiona Coghlan, out-half Lynne Cantwell and Niamh Briggs, Ireland went through the tournament undefeated to claim a first ever Grand Slam title. The following year they went to the World Cup in France and beat New Zealand – known as the Black Ferns in the women's game – for the first time ever and came fourth overall in the tournament, the furthest any senior Irish rugby team had ever gone. Irish women's rugby had arrived.

JOY NEVILLE

Joy Neville is one of the best referees in the world – in men's and women's rugby. And maybe what makes her such a good official is the fact she was one of our top players for many years too. The Limerick woman was skipper of the first Irish women's team to beat France in 2009 and was a key part of the Grand Slam squad four years later. In fact, her last game was the championship clincher in Italy. After she retired, while coaching, Neville was asked if she'd like to try refereeing. She gave it a go and quickly became recognised as an excellent whistle-blower. She's taken charge of top club and international games in both men's and women's tournaments and was named the best referee in the world in 2017.

JACKIE MCCARTHY-O'BRIEN `TRAILBLAZER`

The doubly talented Jackie McCarthy-O'Brien represented Ireland in soccer and rugby – 13 times in each sport, amazingly. The Limerick forward was also the first black female player in either code. Though born in Birmingham in the UK, she moved to Ireland with her mother as a small baby. She lived the first five years of her life in an industrial school run by nuns, which was very hard. McCarthy-O'Brien then returned to her mother and stepfather, a champion handball player, and fell in love with sport. She has always been determined to achieve great things, despite her tough start in life. Her careers in rugby and football helped lead the way for others to follow her.

LINDSAY PEAT

Lindsay Peat was a tough competitor in the No. 1 jersey for Ireland, winning 38 caps after her debut in 2015. Before that, she won an All-Ireland football title with the Dublin footballers, and also represented Ireland at basketball!

☆ GOLDEN AGES ☆

A NEW MILLENNIUM, A NEW ERA

The 1990s was a tough period for Irish rugby. The national team failed to win the Five Nations throughout the decade – in fact they never finished outside the bottom two. But with the introduction of professionalism in 1995 there were signs of hope.

In 1999, we realised we had a star. Twenty-year-old Brian O'Driscoll scored a stunning hat-trick against France to give Ireland their first win in Paris in 28 years. The following year, the under-pressure boss Warren Gatland threw some more young guys into the team. Ronan O'Gara and Peter Stringer sang the anthem in Murrayfield under the big arms of their vastly experienced Munster teammate Mick Galwey. They went out and helped Ireland to a big win against the Scots.

When Eddie O'Sullivan became head coach, he set about introducing more of this new breed of Irish player, our first generation of pros.

Ireland won silverware in 2004, taking the Triple Crown, and the team did the same two years later. The 2007 World Cup was a disappointment, but when the Aviva Stadium was being built, Ireland beat England on a memorable day north of the Liffey.

Declan Kidney, who'd led Munster to two European Cups, replaced O'Sullivan, and in 2009, the team finally achieved their goal of a Six Nations championship, winning a Grand Slam with a thrilling defeat of great rivals Wales in Cardiff.

A decade of struggle and success had established Ireland as one of the best rugby nations in the world.

DID YOU KNOW?

The Five Nations – Ireland, England, Scotland, Wales and France – added Italy in 2000, making it the Six Nations.

✩ GOLDEN AGES ✩

GRAND SLAM GLORIES

THE JOE SCHMIDT ERA

Joe Schmidt travelled from his hometown of Manawatu in New Zealand to play rugby for Mullingar in 1991. He was only 24 but helped coach the team and even lined out for the local GAA team. When he returned home to New Zealand, few would have guessed he'd go on to be Ireland's most successful head coach ever.

Schmidt became an excellent coach and was an assistant at the French club Clermont when Leinster offered him their head coach job.

After a very difficult start, some people called for this unknown Kiwi to be sacked. But Schmidt and the team turned it around. Leinster reached six finals in three years, winning four trophies. The Schmidt era in Ireland had begun.

He took over Ireland in 2013 and set about the biggest job of his career. Under his leadership, Ireland won three Six Nations, including a glorious Grand Slam in 2018.

Schmidt also masterminded the first ever win over his home country, New Zealand, with a famous win at Soldier Field in Chicago in 2016. Two years later, Ireland beat the All Blacks again, capping a special year for Ireland and their boss who was named the best coach in the world. He'd travelled a long way from Manawatu and Mullingar.

IRISH WOMEN 2013-2014

The night before Ireland beat the mighty New Zealand at the 2014 Women's Rugby World Cup, the squad linked arms and sang a song they'd picked up from one of their movie nights. 'Let It Go' from *Frozen* became their anthem. Like Anna and Elsa their story saw them come a long way and overcome great trials.

When many of the players made their debut with Ireland, there wasn't a lot of attention on them. It was mainly friends and family at matches – newspapers or TV stations didn't give the games much coverage. But the players wanted to change things and make a real impact on the pitch.

Philip 'Goose' Doyle was appointed head coach and he set about making the set-up more professional. Players like Fiona Coghlan, Lynne Cantwell and Nora Stapleton were part of a group with big personalities and things started to improve.

In 2013, they went on a run in the Six Nations, beating England for the first time ever and setting up a championship decider in Italy. RTÉ broadcast the game – it was the first time a women's rugby game was shown live on the national broadcaster. They finally won the championship and then asked, 'What's next?' The following year at the World Cup, they beat the Black Ferns and made it to the last four of the World Cup for the first time. Irish women's rugby was at the top of the global game at last.

GREATEST IRISH RUGBY PLAYERS

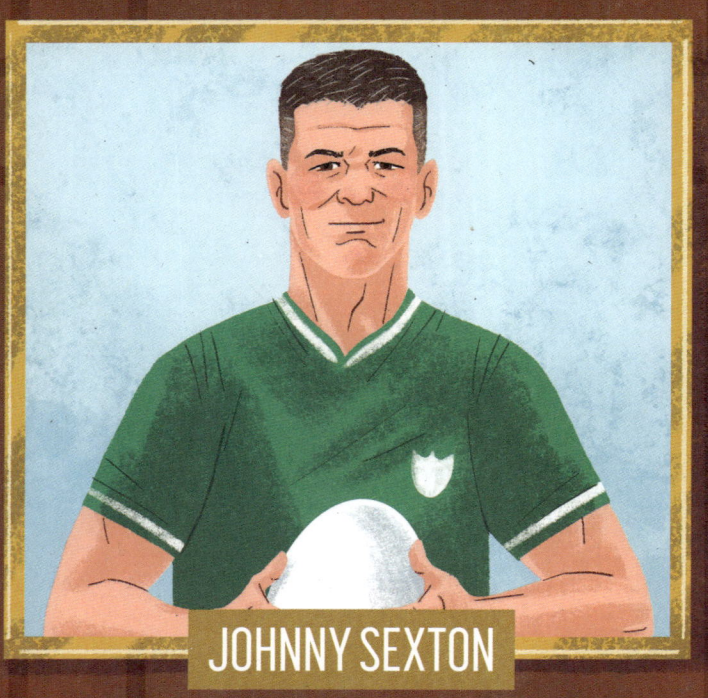

JOHNNY SEXTON

Johnny Sexton has been Ireland's most important men's player during their most successful era. Since he won the No. 10 jersey, he's been the general at out-half for the national team, kicking over 1,000 points in his test career. Sexton helped Leinster to four Champions Cup victories and was named World Player of the Year in 2018. He vowed to retire after Ireland's World Cup 2023 campaign in France.

FIONA COGHLAN

Fiona Coghlan is our most important women's rugby player ever. A sports-mad kid, Coghlan initially liked horse riding and tennis – rugby sadly wasn't as much of an option for girls in the 1990s. In her first week of university, she signed up to try rugby. Within a few years she was leading Irish rugby into a golden era.

In 2013, Coghlan led Ireland to an amazing Grand Slam triumph. When they beat England 34-0, the media and public took proper notice of Irish women's rugby for the first time. A year later, they beat the All Blacks in the World Cup and made it to the last four.

BRIAN O'DRISCOLL

Rugby enthusiasts in Ireland suspected Brian O'Driscoll was going to be special, but he announced himself to the world with a stunning display in Paris in 2000. Ireland hadn't won in Paris in 28 years, but O'Driscoll scored a hat trick of tries to record a famous win at Stade de France.

He'd yet to play for Leinster, but forced his way into the Ireland side at just 20. It set the tone for a career in which he'd go on to be arguably our greatest ever player. He was fast, strong and highly intelligent – equally talented in attack and defence – and won multiple honours with Ireland and Leinster.

PAUL O'CONNELL

'Did you put the fear of God into them?' Paul O'Connell asked his teammates at Croke Park as Ireland faced England. O'Connell put the fear of God into teams all over the world during a superb career that saw him captain Ireland, Munster and the Lions. He was Ireland's most capped player when he retired, having won multiple Six Nations championships and European Cups.

LYNNE CANTWELL

Lynne Cantwell won 86 caps for Ireland over a 13-year period that saw the game here and the national team transform. Cantwell's first love was track and field – she was a talented 400m runner, before drifting from athletics to rugby and being fast-tracked into the national set-up. The Dubliner went on to be a Grand Slam winner and represented Ireland at four World Cups.

RONAN O'GARA

O'Gara was out-half for Munster during their glory years and kicked Ireland to many wins during a glittering playing career. He retired as Ireland's record scorer having totted up over, 1000 points. O'Gara featured for the Lions and was widely considered one of the best players in the game during his career. He's now a very highly rated coach, having led La Rochelle to two European titles – the French club's first silverware ever.

TONY WARD

Tony Ward was an exciting out-half with Ireland, winning 19 caps and earning a Lions call-up. Ward also inspired Munster in their legendary 1978 win over the All Blacks, scoring two drop goals and a conversion in a 12–0 victory at Thomond Park. He also played for Shamrock Rovers and Limerick City, helping them to the FAI Cup, as well as lining out in Europe with them.

JACK KYLE

When Ireland won the Grand Slam in 2009, Brian O'Driscoll went to Jack Kyle in the Millennium Stadium crowd to celebrate. Kyle was an important part of the last Irish side to achieve a Grand Slam back in 1948. He was inducted into the International Hall of Fame and was named Ireland's greatest-ever player by the IRFU in 2002. The Belfast native was a hugely talented out-half and won 48 Irish caps, as well as representing the Barbarians and Lions.

NIAMH BRIGGS

Niamh Briggs was a big part of the Ireland women's team that made their breakthrough after years of hard work. The Waterford woman starred for the county's Gaelic football team but concentrated on rugby and earned her place at No. 10 with Ireland. In 2013, when Ireland won their first Grand Slam and Six Nations, Briggs was top scorer for the tournament. She's now a top-level coach, guiding the next generation of Ireland players through.

KEITH WOOD

Keith Wood was always a leader and a class player during some tough years for Ireland. Ever recognisable as he stormed around the pitch, Wood was hugely skilled in the important hooker position. He starred for the British and Irish Lions, was key in the evolution of his home province, Munster, and was the first winner of the World Player of the Year Award in 2001.

A HISTORY OF BOXING IN IRELAND

Ding-dong! Seconds out! Let's get ready to rumble!

Boxing is one of the oldest combat sports in the world, and Ireland has a rich history in the so-called 'sweet science' at all levels of the sport, with Olympic champions in the amateur ranks and lots of world champions in the pro game.

Before the 1850s boxing took place without gloves and few standard rules. However, with the introduction of the Queensberry rules in 1867, the sport began to be regulated. In the late 19th century, the first boxing clubs began to open up around Ireland. The IABA – which organises the amateur sport here – was founded in 1911. It wasn't long before they made the bold move to build the National Stadium in Dublin. Soon, Ireland established itself as a country that produced skilful and brave fighters.

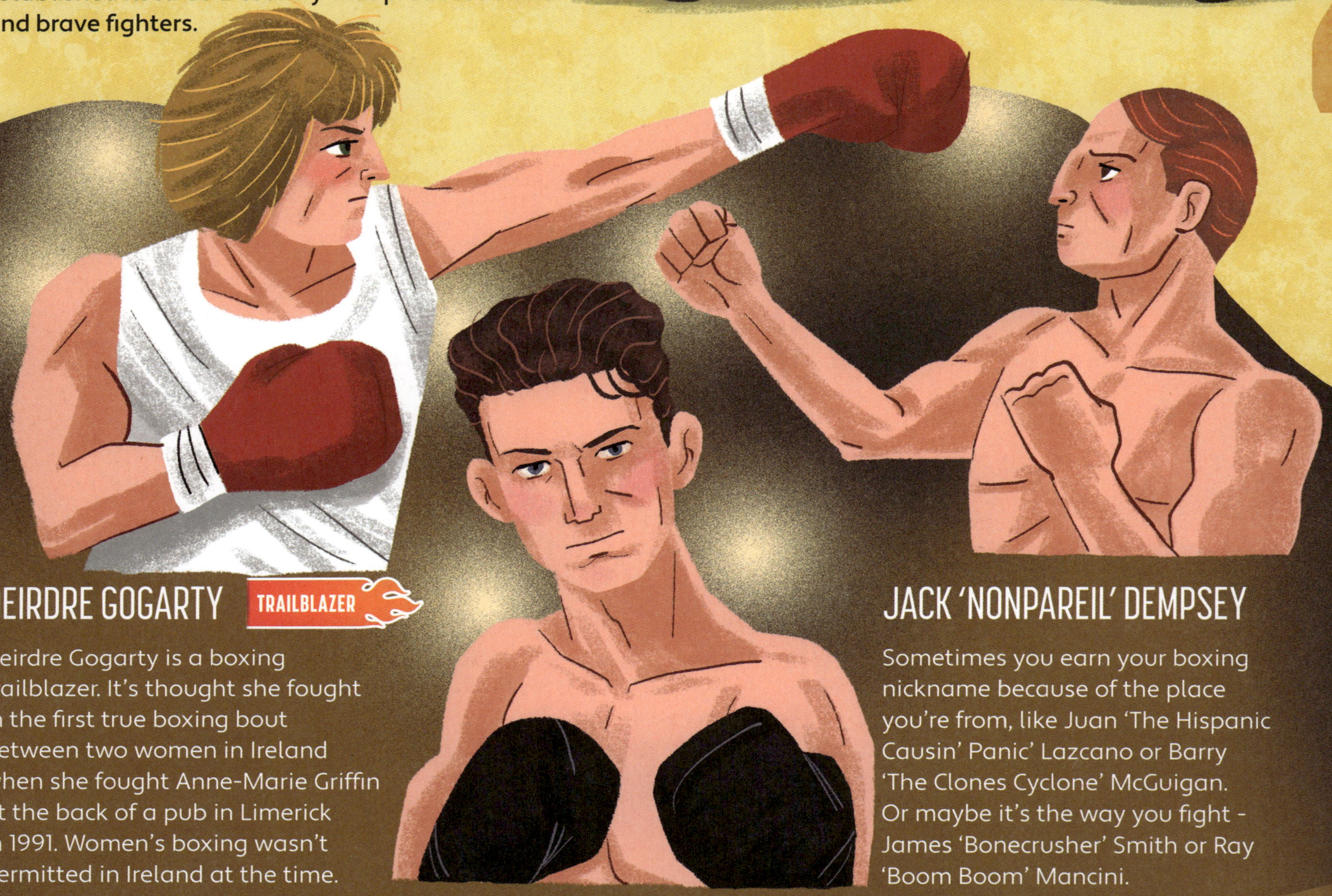

DEIRDRE GOGARTY — TRAILBLAZER

Deirdre Gogarty is a boxing trailblazer. It's thought she fought in the first true boxing bout between two women in Ireland when she fought Anne-Marie Griffin at the back of a pub in Limerick in 1991. Women's boxing wasn't permitted in Ireland at the time.

A few years later she broke more barriers for women boxers, fighting in Las Vegas as part of the first women's fight on a pay-per-view show. She is Ireland's first-ever female world champion, and she punched through the glass ceiling for the stars that followed her.

JACK DOYLE

The 'Gorgeous Gael' Jack Doyle led an amazing life. The Cobh man was a great heavyweight and afterwards became a famous tenor singer, tried acting and even married a Hollywood starlet.

JACK 'NONPAREIL' DEMPSEY

Sometimes you earn your boxing nickname because of the place you're from, like Juan 'The Hispanic Causin' Panic' Lazcano or Barry 'The Clones Cyclone' McGuigan. Or maybe it's the way you fight - James 'Bonecrusher' Smith or Ray 'Boom Boom' Mancini.

Jack Dempsey earned his nickname because he was the best – 'Nonpareil' translates as 'without equal'. Dempsey was born in 1862 in Kildare and went on to win the world middleweight title in New York – he held the title for six years before he died far too young at just 32.

WEIGHT CLASSES

When the rules of boxing were set out, lots of weight divisions were agreed. This was to make sure boxers fought opponents of roughly their own size. More divisions have been added over the years – today there are 17 in the pro game.

These range from super heavyweight to middleweight, welterweight and strawweight, with loads in between.

In big fights, the boxers have to be under the agreed weight and are weighed the day before the bout. Sometimes they have to work really hard to 'make weight' and do crazy things like go running while dressed in bin liners to sweat off some pounds!

JIMMY MCLARNIN

Jimmy McLarnin emigrated from Co. Down to Canada as a child and was soon spotted by a shrewd boxing man, Charles 'Pop' Foster.

A series of big wins, including huge fights at Madison Square Garden in New York, saw Jimmy adopted as the Irish-American favourite. He had lots of nicknames, like the 'Babyface Assassin', and became an undisputed champion of the world at welterweight in 1933. He retired at 31 as an all-time great and led a happy life with his family until he died at 95.

ALI AT CROKE PARK

Croke Park has been home to the GAA for over a century. But it also hosted the boxer known as 'The Greatest', Muhammad Ali. Ali was known for his style in the ring, his way with words and iconic victories in blockbuster fights like the 'Thrilla in Manila' and the 'Rumble in the Jungle'.

Ali – who changed his name from Cassius Clay when he converted to Islam, becoming a Muslim – fought Al 'Blue' Lewis in Dublin in 1973. The former heavyweight champ beat Lewis in the 11th round, and the corner of Croke Park where Ali emerged for the bout is still known as the Ali Tunnel today.

49

HALL OF FAME

KATIE TAYLOR

Katie Taylor is possibly Ireland's greatest ever sportsperson. As a young girl in Bray, Co. Wicklow, Taylor played lots of sports – she even lined out for Ireland's women's soccer team. She loved boxing most, however, even though there weren't lots of opportunities for girls to take part in tournaments. Coached by her dad, Pete, Taylor often hid her ponytail in her headgear and fought – and beat – boys in the ring. She won world titles as an amateur and her impressive performances were one of the main reasons that women's boxing was added to the Olympics in 2012. Eventually she went professional and soon became undisputed champion of the world while inspiring the next generation of boxers and athletes in Ireland and around the globe.

KELLIE HARRINGTON

Kellie Harrington had to work and battle hard to get to the top. From Dublin's north inner city, she says she could have chosen a bad path in life if it wasn't for boxing. The clubs in her area were for boys only and she had to fight to be allowed to join.

She showed lots of promise but wasn't a star initially. Harrington struggled in some competitions and didn't think she was supported enough by those in charge of the sport here. In fact, she often thought of giving up. She kept going, though, and persevered to become a world and Olympic champion, earning her place as one of Ireland's most beloved sports stars and a boxing great.

STEVE COLLINS

The 'Celtic Warrior' was a two-weight world champion who took on some of the biggest names in boxing in the 1990s. The Dubliner moved to the US and started to make a name for himself in Boston as a pro but won his first title when he relocated to England. He moved up to the glamorous super middleweight division and dethroned champion Chris Eubank. He had famous fights with Nigel Benn which underlined his class. Collins never lost the belt in the ring – instead he was stripped of the strap because he backed out of a fight with Joe Calzaghe due to injury. Collins retired soon after, a legend of Irish professional boxing.

BARRY MCGUIGAN

When the Troubles in Northern Ireland were at their most violent, Barry McGuigan insisted that he fought for everyone in the country. The featherweight from Clones in Co. Monaghan wore the peace symbol of the dove and the flag of the United Nations on his shorts. He represented Northern Ireland at the Commonwealth Games and Ireland at the Olympics. As a pro, McGuigan won the hearts of everyone for his battling displays in the ring and was one of Ireland's biggest stars in the 1980s.

HONOURABLE MENTIONS

WAYNE MCCULLOUGH: The 'Pocket Rocket' McCullough was an exciting fighter from Belfast who became a world champion at bantamweight after he won a silver medal for Ireland at the 1992 Olympics.

DEIRDRE GOGARTY: Gogarty led the way for the likes of Katie Taylor, Kellie Harrington and Christina Desmond. She was Ireland's first female world boxing champion.

DAVE 'BOY' MCAULEY: McAuley won a world title at the third time of asking in 1989. The Larne fighter is regarded as one of our greatest ever flyweights.

ANDY LEE: A stylish middleweight from Limerick, Lee represented Ireland at the 2004 Olympics and became the first Traveller to win a world title after he turned professional.

RINTY MONAGHAN: Fighting in the post-war era, John 'Rinty' Monaghan was an undisputed world champion and earned a statue in his proud hometown of Belfast.

BERNARD DUNNE: The Dubliner had a superb professional boxing career at super bantamweight, winning 28 of 30 fights. When he got a chance at a world title he beat Ricardo Cordoba at a packed Point Depot in 2009. Ireland had won a famous rugby Grand Slam hours beforehand and the arena was rocking. Dunne went on to be Irish boxing's high performance director and has worked with Dublin GAA.

IRELAND'S GREATEST BOXING MOMENTS

BARRY MCGUIGAN V EUSEBIO PEDROZA, 1985

Barry McGuigan won lots of fans for his brave fighting, likeable personality and determination to represent everyone on the island of Ireland. He eventually earned a world title shot against Eusebio Pedroza at the football ground of London soccer club QPR. Nearly 30,000 people crowded in to see McGuigan's father sing 'Danny Boy' in the ring before his son won the belt after 15 gruelling rounds. McGuigan only managed to hang on to the title for a year before losing it to Steve Cruz in the Las Vegas heat in 1986, but the Loftus Road victory was a shining light during dark times for Irish people.

MICHAEL CARRUTH, BARCELONA 1992

In 1992, Ireland hadn't won a gold medal at the Olympics since Ronnie Delany in 1956. Michael Carruth, a soldier from Dublin, put an end to the wait. Carruth was a triplet and one of 10 children in total.

In the army, he was allowed to train as a boxer every day, representing the armed forces in boxing tournaments. He got to the Olympics for Ireland in 1988 but was beaten in his second fight when he was knocked down for the first and last time in his career. When he got back to the barracks, some fellow soldiers made fun of his performance. 'Those comments hurt as much as any punch,' he said. 'I had to get back to the Olympics.'

Four years later, in Barcelona '92, he would make it all the way to the final. Carruth battled against a stylish Cuban boxer called Juan Hernández. Even though he actually broke both his own hands in the fight, the Dubliner won the bout 13-10 to make history for Ireland.

KATIE TAYLOR, LONDON 2012

By 2011 Katie Taylor was the best female fighter in the world, but women's boxing wasn't part of the Olympics. After a long campaign, it was finally introduced for the 2012 Olympics in London and the whole world expected Taylor to win a history-making gold medal for Ireland. The pressure was on.

Lots of Irish fans filled the specially built new arena, the Excel, and cheered the Bray woman on throughout the tournament. She managed to get to the final where she'd face the Russian Sofya Ochigava. Taylor said she didn't sleep very well the night before. It was a really close fight. The Russian fighter had performed very well and expected to be announced as the winner. When Taylor was declared the champion at women's boxing's first Olympics she dropped to her knees and pointed to the sky.

'It was my childhood dream coming to pass,' she said later.

STEVE COLLINS V CHRIS EUBANK, 1995

Lots of Irish boxing's most memorable nights took place in famous venues like Madison Square Garden in New York or huge stadiums throughout the world. One very special victory, however, happened in a horse-jumping arena in rural Co. Cork!

Dublin's Steve Collins dethroned the champion Chris Eubank at a packed Green Glens Arena in Millstreet to be crowned the WBO Super Middleweight Champion of the World in 1995. Eubank was a brilliant champion and had been undefeated going into the fight, but the 'Celtic Warrior' Collins pulled off an upset.

The two fighters met in a rematch at the home of Cork GAA, Páirc Uí Chaoimh, later in the same year. Collins claimed to be hypnotised so he could perform better. Maybe it worked, as Collins won again and Eubank retired from boxing soon afterwards.

KELLIE HARRINGTON, TOKYO 2020 IN 2021

'Hakuna matata!' Kellie Harrington said after she secured a bronze medal at the delayed 2020 Tokyo Olympics. The phrase from the *Lion King* means 'no worries' and the Dublin boxer was keeping cool as she faced two more fights to clinch an Olympic gold.

It had been a long road for Harrington. She wasn't an established star like Katie Taylor – who fought at the same weight – but she trained hard and was determined to make her mark. She won a world title in 2018 and set her sights on the Olympics. She had to wait an extra year for the Games to take place because of COVID-19 but she was determined to make history by becoming the second Irishwoman to win an Olympic gold medal in boxing.

She boxed cleverly all the way to the final. The street where she came from, Portland Row, was decked out in green, white and gold. The whole country got up early that Sunday morning to watch her big moment. After a tough fight, she collapsed to her knees when the ref went to the red corner to declare her as the new lightweight Olympic champion. No worries.

A HISTORY OF HORSE RACING IN IRELAND

And they're off! Ireland is one of the leading countries in the world for producing top-class jockeys, trainers and – most importantly – horses in what's known as the 'Sport of Kings'. Horse racing – in various forms – is one of our oldest sports. Chariot and bareback racing were held in the first Olympics. In Ireland, our legends describe Fionn MacCumhaill and his men racing their horses across the Curragh, and manuscripts tell us of chariot racing on the Kildare plains.

Racing here became more organised in the 17th century under King Charles II, an enthusiastic patron of the sport. He introduced King's Plates races, which were fiercely contested. In the mid-18th century, the first body for Irish racing was formed in a Dublin pub. The Society of Sportsmen later became the Irish Jockey Club and then the Turf Club.

JUMP RACING

We in Ireland are especially adept at jump racing, the type of races where the horses have obstacles to get over. There are two types of obstacles: hurdles and fences. Also called National Hunt, these races take place all year round and are usually run over a distance of two miles up to four miles and a furlong.

FLAT RACING

Flat races go over five furlongs to two miles and the horses and jockeys don't need to worry about getting over any obstacles. The races usually take place on grass but Dundalk has an all-weather track. There are 26 racecourses in Ireland but you might see 'point-to-point' races on beaches like Laytown in Co. Meath too.

WHAT'S THE 'GOING'?

The ground on which the horses run is vital to how a race can go. The 'going' is the description given to the ground at racecourses. There are several types of going:

FIRM: This is often seen during the summer season. A firmer track can mean a faster race. It can also be more dangerous for jockeys and horses who fall.

GOOD: This is the most common type of ground and suits the most horses.

SOFT: Often seen during the wetter jumps season, soft ground can suit certain horses.

THE LINGO

From the equipment to the horses to gambling on a race's outcome, horse racing has a language of its own.

A FURLONG: Distances in racing are often measured in furlongs – it's 220 yards, or one-eighth of a mile.

NOSEBAND: A sheepskin band that goes over a horse's nose to help it concentrate.

BLINKERS: The piece of equipment that goes over a horse's head to reduce distractions during a race.

SILKS: The name for the colourful uniforms worn by the jockeys. Each owner of a horse has their own distinctive pattern and colours.

BRIDLE: The equipment on a horse's head to allow the jockey to control it.

BIT: The metal part of the bridle that sits in the horse's mouth. It's where we get the phrase 'champing at the bit'.

THE GRAND NATIONAL

The Grand National at Aintree Racecourse in Liverpool is one of the most famous races in the world. Racing experts often say the race is something of a lottery; it's hard to pick a winner and favourites often fall on the way around the challenging course. In total there are 16 fences on the course, but horses have to jump 14 of them twice. There are several famous fences like Becher's Brook and Canal Turn. The highest is The Chair at 5 foot 2 inches, with a 5 foot ditch on the jumping side!

THE IRISH GRAND NATIONAL

The Irish Grand National has a rich history of its own, of course, and is run each Easter Monday at Fairyhouse racecourse.

THE CHELTENHAM FESTIVAL

Every year a town in the Cotswolds in England hosts what jump experts call 'Racing's Olympics'. The National Hunt season in the UK and Ireland is geared towards the biggest races at Prestbury Park in March, especially the famous Cheltenham Gold Cup. Irish trainers and owners put their best horses in trailers and on ferries to take on the best horses from Britain. In recent years Ireland has dominated the festival and taken what is now called the 'Prestbury Cup', which is contested by the Irish and UK camps. Thousands of Irish racing enthusiasts travel over to Cheltenham each year to see the action and roar on the 'raiders'.

THE FIRST STEEPLECHASE

Jumps races are also called steeplechases around the world, but how did they get that name? The first of these races is said to have taken place between the 'steeples' of the churches in Buttevant and Doneraile in Co. Cork in 1752.

THE GREATEST IRISH HORSES

ARKLE

Arkle is remembered fondly by racing fans as the greatest steeplechaser of all time. Trained by Tom Dreaper and ridden by Pat Taafe, he won three Cheltenham Gold Cups, the 1964 Grand National and loads of other races in Ireland and the UK. And he often carried a heavy handicap while doing it. He retired, because of injury, at the age of nine and is now commemorated with a large bronze statue in his native Co. Meath. You can also see his preserved skeleton at the National Stud in Kildare.

DAWN RUN — TRAILBLAZER

Dawn Run was a mare who was able to compete against the best males in the brutally competitive jumps. Trained by Paddy Mullins, she's arguably the greatest mare to ever race and is the only horse of either gender to pull off a historic double. She won the 1984 Champion Hurdle and the 1986 Gold Cup. Sadly, she fell in a race in France and died tragically. Her death was front-page news the following day.

VINTAGE CROP

Australia is a long way away. It was even longer in 1993 and the journey was much tougher if you were a thoroughbred racehorse. Vintage Crop – trained by Dermot Weld – won 16 races on these islands between 1992 and '95. But his victory at the prestigious Melbourne Cup made history. The Irish star was the first overseas horse to achieve the win at 'the race that stops a nation'.

WHAT'S A STUD FARM?

Breeding of horses is really important and is big business. Racehorses who have had successful careers often produce the next generation of champions. Stallions are sent to 'stud farms' where they are paired with mares in the hope they will produce a foal, who'll hopefully go on to thrill horse-racing lovers in the future.

WHAT'S A HANDICAP?

In handicap races, the best horses have to carry extra weight that's added to their equipment. It means that races are more even and exciting. An official called a handicapper decides how much extra weight a horse should carry to make the race more competitive.

> **DID YOU KNOW?**
> **THE WEIGHING ROOM**
> The weighing room is one of the most important places on a racecourse. Jockeys are weighed before each meeting and the room where this happens is where they get ready for races together, chat about what's happened and recover before they have to get in a saddle again.

RED RUM

Red Rum was born in Kells, Co. Kilkenny, and after several years of moving from one owner to another, he was bought as a crippled seven-year-old and nursed to full health by his trainer Ginger McCain, who ran him in seawater to help his hooves. The Irish steeplechaser went on to be one of the most famous horses ever – winning the Grand National an unprecedented three times, in 1973, '74 and '77. He was known for his wonderful jumping and never fell in over 100 races. When he died in 1995, he was buried at the winning post at Aintree and racegoers still visit the grave of the horse today.

ISTABRAQ

A beloved hurdler who's an all-time great and a 25-time winner, trained by Aidan O'Brien, Istabraq's three consecutive Champion Hurdles (1998, '99 and '00) and four Irish Champion Hurdles are legendary. After his retirement, the gelding was moved to the home of his owner J.P. McManus.

SEA THE STARS

The Irish thoroughbred racehorse Sea the Stars is considered by many as amongst the greatest racehorses ever. He won the Derby, the 2000 Guineas, the Irish Champion Stakes and even the Prix de l'Arc de Triomphe in France.

THE MYSTERY OF SHERGAR

Shergar was an Irish-bred thoroughbred racehorse who was owned by the Aga Khan. He won big races like the Epsom Derby and the Irish Derby before he retired to a stud in Kildare in 1981. He was stolen from the stud, however, and the kidnappers demanded a massive £2 million ransom to release him. The money wasn't paid and Shergar was never found.

> **DIFFERENT NAMES FOR HORSES**
>
> **FILLY:**
> A female horse aged up to four years old.
>
> **MARE:**
> A female horse aged five years or older.
>
> **GELDING:**
> A male horse not required for breeding.
>
> **COLT:**
> A male horse up to five years old.
>
> **STALLION:**
> A male breeding horse.

GREATEST IRISH JOCKEYS AND TRAINERS

RUBY WALSH

Ruby Walsh had a spectacular start to his career and didn't let up. At the age of 20, he won the Aintree Grand National in 2000 on Papillon, trained by his father, Ted. He went on to be AP McCoy's great rival and challenged him throughout his career. Walsh was born into a famous horse-racing family - his father was a great amateur jockey and a trainer and is a much-loved TV pundit. Ruby's sister Kate blazed a trail for female riders, as did his sister-in-law, Nina Carbery. Walsh loved the big races and had 59 winners at Cheltenham with two Gold Cup wins in 2007 and 2009 with Kauto Star.

AP MCCOY

Sometimes kids are told they're too small to be the sports star they'd like to be. Anthony 'AP' McCoy thought he was too *tall* to be a jockey. Born in Co. Antrim, he moved to Jim Bolger's yard at 15 to try to make it. He then established himself in England and, by winning races from the age of 17, made a reputation as one of the top riders in Britain and Ireland. McCoy was known for his toughness, suffering lots of broken bones and other injuries throughout his long career. But he always got back on the horse. He was champion jockey many times and when he retired in 2015 he had notched an incredible 4,357 victories.

RACHAEL BLACKMORE

In 2021, Rachael Blackmore became the first female jockey to win the Aintree Grand National in the 182-year history of the race. She also became the first woman to be leading jockey at the Cheltenham Festival with six victories, including the Champion Hurdle, in 2021. The following year the Tipperary woman became the first female jockey to win the Cheltenham Gold Cup. Blackmore's ground-breaking achievements made her the 2021 RTÉ Sports Person of the Year and even the BBC's World Sport Star of the Year.

NINA CARBERRY

TRAILBLAZER

One of the best amateur riders ever, Nina Carberry broke barriers over a successful 17-year career. She won seven times at the Cheltenham Festival and she was the first female jump jockey in Ireland and Britain to win a Grade 1 race when winning at Punchestown in 2006. Carberry comes from a well-known racing family and she emulated her father and brothers when riding the winner of the 2011 Irish Grand National on Organisedconfusion.

GORDON ELLIOTT

Gordon Elliott began his career in racing as a teenager, working in a local yard at weekends. He went on to become the youngest trainer ever to win the Aintree Grand National at the age of 29 in 2007. The brilliant Tiger Roll gave the Meath man his second success at the famous race when winning under Davy Russell in 2018. Tiger Roll and Russell won the race *again* the following year to make history: he was the first horse to win the race back-to-back since Red Rum in 1973 and 1974.

VINCENT O'BRIEN

One the best trainers in the world for 50 years, Vincent O'Brien was a successful jockey from Cork before establishing the now world-famous Ballydoyle training centre in Tipperary in the 1950s. He won all the major National Hunt races, including three Grand Nationals on the trot and four Cheltenham Gold Cups. When he switched to flat racing he had even greater success, training winners in lots of prestigious races. Nijinsky's Triple Crown success in 1970 was probably the crowning glory. He partnered with the prolific jockey Lestor Piggott, who rode many winners for him, and Ballydoyle is still producing great horses today, under Aidan O'Brien.

HENRY DE BROMHEAD

Since the Waterford man took over his father's yard in the late 1990s he's built it into a destination for some of our top horses. De Bromhead is the only trainer to have won the Champion Hurdle, Champion Chase and the Gold Cup at the Cheltenham Festival in the same year. He's enjoyed a fruitful partnership with jockey Rachael Blackmore. A few weeks after his record-setting Cheltenham Festival success in 2021, he won the Aintree Grand National with the Blackmore-ridden Minella Times.

WILLIE MULLINS

Willie Mullins is our most successful trainer. He leads the way in the all-time trainer standings at Cheltenham with a huge 88 winners, so far. He'll always be associated with a horse he thinks is one of the best ever. The legendary Hurricane Fly won 24 of his 32 starts over hurdles and in doing so notched up a world-record-breaking 22 victories at Grade 1 level over a glorious 10-year career.

IRELAND AND THE OLYMPICS

Every four years, the world's best athletes gather in one city to compete in events like sprinting, swimming and boxing. As well as the Summer Olympic Games, the top athletes on snow and ice take part in the Winter Games separately. The prize is glory for your country, your place in history and a medal: bronze, silver or gold for the event winner.

OLYMPIC HISTORY

The first known ancient Olympic Games were held in 776BC at a sacred place, Olympia in Greece. The Olympics were held to honour the god Zeus, and though Greek cities and states were often at war, they put their differences aside to take part in the events. At that time, only men were allowed to compete, and they took part completely naked!

CHANGING WITH THE TIMES

Some of the events we see on our screens today were present at the first games – like running and wrestling. But there are lots of things that are different – we no longer try chariot racing or fighting to the death, thankfully – and many new sports have been added, like BMX racing and gymnastics.

THE OLYMPIC FLAG

The flag of the Olympic Games has five linked rings on a white background. The rings represent the five parts of the world linked together by the Games. They're blue, yellow, black, green and red – at least one of the colours appears in every country's flag.

THE OLYMPIC MOTTO

After the Romans banned the Games, around 400AD, we didn't have an Olympics for nearly 1,500 years. A Frenchman, Pierre de Coubertin, revived them in the late 1800s, and introduced the motto for the Modern Olympics: *Citius, altius, fortius* – faster, higher, stronger. The Winter Olympics were added later, in 1924.

IRELAND'S OLYMPIC HISTORY

The first Irish-born winner of an Olympic gold medal was Dubliner John Pius Boland, who won the tennis singles event in Athens in 1896. There were lots of Irish-born medallists in the early years of the Olympics but they often represented countries like the US, Canada and, of course, the UK.

However, Ireland was given formal recognition in 1924 and at the Paris Games that year we made our first appearance at an Olympic Games as an independent nation.

Ireland didn't win any medals in the French capital in the sporting events, but back then there were other events that we excelled in. The famous painter Jack B. Yeats won a silver medal for his painting *The Liffey Swim* in the art competition – the first Olympic medal for the Irish Free State – and Oliver St John Gogarty won bronze in the literature event for his poem 'Ode to the Tailteann Games'. Would this book win gold at the Olympics? Almost certainly.

DID YOU KNOW?
Athletes from more than 200 different countries compete in the Olympics.

MARTIN SHERIDAN

Martin Sheridan was born in Bohola, Co. Leitrim in 1881. It wasn't long before his great strength was noticed as a child. He emigrated, like many Irish people at that time, to New York and joined the police force. In his spare time he excelled in many sports. Representing the US in the first modern Olympics, which were held in St Louis, he claimed gold in the discus. He won two more gold medals in London and refused to lower his flag, as instructed, when passing the King of England. He was hailed as one of the best athletes in America but sadly died of pneumonia at just 37 years old.

LADY HEATH

Sophie Mary Peirce-Evans started her life in Limerick in 1896, but would go on to be known worldwide by a different name. Lady Mary Heath was a renowned aviator who piloted on record-breaking aeroplane journeys to prove that women could fly planes too. She was the first woman ever to fly over the equator. Peirce-Evans became Lady Heath when she married an English politician. She was also an accomplished athlete and set world records in the javelin and high jump. Just like in aviation, she had to prove that women deserved their place at the Olympics, and eventually she helped gymnastics be included in 1928.

DR PAT O'CALLAGHAN

O'Callaghan claimed Ireland's first gold medal as an independent nation in 1928 with a surprise win in the hammer event in Amsterdam. He was new to the sport and didn't expect to make an impact but won the whole thing. He proved his class at the Games in Los Angeles in 1932 when he claimed gold again.

RONNIE DELANY

Ronnie Delany was the surprise Olympic champion in the 1,500m in Melbourne in 1956. The Wicklow man set an Olympic record as he raced across the finish line, having undergone a long journey to get to Australia. People back home in Ireland learned of the amazing victory on the radio at breakfast time.

ATHELETES ON THE WORLD STAGE

SONIA O'SULLIVAN

Sonia O'Sullivan is one of Ireland's most successful and well-known athletes. In fact, she is so beloved and respected for her achievements on the running track that most people in Ireland just call her 'Sonia'.

All over the country, sports fans made sure to be in front of their television sets when she ran her biggest races. Everyone knew that the Cobh woman liked to run in the middle of the pack until the end of the race, when she'd 'kick' and race away from everyone.

She won lots of races and medals but also had disappointments and losses. The people of Ireland loved her because of the way she always tried her hardest and always came back stronger from setbacks.

Representing Ireland, Sonia *just* missed out on the podium at her first Olympics at Barcelona '92. She looked like she'd win gold but was passed out on the final bend. Coming fourth in her final, she cried afterwards but knew she'd made it to the big time and would be back.

A year later, Sonia was beaten in the 3,000m world championship final by three runners from China. Their trainer said the secret to their success was a concoction of turtle blood and caterpillar fungus! Sonia overcame her disappointment to brilliantly win silver in the 1,500m final a few days later, though. It made her the first Irishwoman to medal at a World Championships.

DID YOU KNOW?

You can visit a statue of Sonia in her hometown of Cobh in east Cork. The statue was created by James McLoughlin and was put up by the people of the town in 2015. It shows Sonia with her hands in the air as she crosses the imaginary line to win ... again!

DID YOU KNOW?

Ireland has produced world champions in athletics in John Treacy, Eamonn Coghlan, Marcus O'Sullivan, Frank O'Mara, Derval O'Rourke and Robert Heffernan.

The girl from Cork became a world champion in 1995 by winning the first-ever running of the women's 5,000m in Gothenburg. Sonia was now the best around and her races were appointment television. (Recording television was a lot harder in those days!) A year later, at her next Olympics in Atlanta, O'Sullivan was really sick, not in good form and had a hard time. The whole country was very disappointed that Sonia missed her big chance at gold, but she again promised that she'd be back.

A little over a year after her first daughter, Ciara, was born, Sonia O'Sullivan lined up on the start line of the 5,000m final at the Sydney Olympics in 2000. Though she was no longer the very best in the sport, everyone hoped this was her chance to finally win an Olympic medal.

The race came down to a battle between Ireland and Romania – Sonia versus her great rival, Gabrielle Szabo. Would Sonia be able to 'kick for home' and run for the line really strongly to claim the gold?

'When I came up on Gabrielle's shoulder I felt she'd gone as well as she could and I thought I had it,' Sonia said afterwards. 'But she just moved up a little bit and that was it.' Szabo broke the Olympic record, and Sonia took the Irish record in an amazing race. It was an Olympic medal – a silver – for Sonia O'Sullivan at last in Sydney. Back home, over breakfast, the Irish people celebrated an Irish sporting legend.

CIARA MAGEEAN

Ciara Mageean is running in Sonia O'Sullivan's footsteps in races like the 1,500m. Growing up she dreamed of playing camogie for Co. Down but her natural running ability marked her apart. She sometimes gives so much during her races that she throws up in the middle of TV interviews straight afterwards! Mageean has won medals at European championships and is gunning to make the podium in Paris in 2024.

EAMONN COGHLAN

Because of his dominance at indoor races, Eamonn Coghlan was known as 'the Chairman of the Boards'. In 1983, he set an incredible world indoor mile record of 3:49.78 and later in the summer claimed the first world championship 5,000m title with a perfectly run race. He finished fourth in the 1,500m at the Montreal Olympics and four years later finished fourth again in the 5,000m at the Moscow Olympics. Though he finished his career without the Olympic medal it deserved, his stunning performances mean he's a legend of Irish athletics.

IRISH ATHLETES ACROSS THE OLYMPICS

NATALYA COYLE – MODERN PENTATHLON

The modern pentathlon is an Olympic event made up of five different sports – fencing, freestyle swimming, showjumping, pistol shooting and cross-country running. It's really difficult – imagine training for five different sports at once! Ireland had never had a female pentathlete at the Games until Natalya Coyle from Meath qualified for the London Games. She finished ninth even though she was just 20 years old. Coyle was part of the Ireland team at two more Olympics and won a world silver medal before retiring.

CIAN O'CONNOR – EQUESTRIAN

Cian O'Connor won the bronze medal in individual jumping on his horse Blue Loyd 12 at the London Olympics in 2012. At that stage, he was well known in Ireland for his Olympic performances. Eight years earlier in Athens, O'Connor, riding the horse Waterford Crystal, took the gold. It was Ireland's only medal of the entire Olympic Games. However, later that year it emerged Waterford Crystal had failed a drugs test. Though it was found O'Connor did not deliberately try to improve the horse's performance, he was stripped of the medal.

IRELAND'S WOMEN'S HOCKEY TEAM

Ireland's women's hockey team were heartbroken when they missed out on Olympic qualification in 2012 and 2016. It seemed like they'd always *just* lose out. But in 2018 at the World Cup in London, the lowest ranked team went on an incredible run through the tournament. Part-time players, they were inspired by their almost unbeatable goalkeeper Ayeisha McFerran and led by skipper Katie Mullan. They got to the World Cup final and ultimately took the silver medal. The performance inspired them to go on and at last seal Olympic qualification. In a playoff, they faced a dramatic penalty shootout against Canada to reach Tokyo. Roisin Upton scored to force sudden death before McFerran saved to seal Ireland's first ever hockey place at the Olympic Games.

THE WINTER OLYMPICS

While the Summer Olympic Games feature track races, swimming and boxing, the Winter Games have lots of other sports. Held every four years too, you can expect to see sports like figure skating, snowboarding and ice hockey.

The first organised winter sports competition was known as the Nordic Games and featured countries like Norway and Sweden before it eventually became part of the Olympic cycle.

ROBERT HEFFERNAN – RACE WALKING

In most races, the aim is to just get to the finish line as fast as possible. In race walking, you have to do that in a very particular way. Competitors must always have one foot in contact with the ground. Judges keep an eye on the race walkers and can warn them if they think they've broken the rules and even disqualify them. Try it. It's really tough physically and technically and at the Olympics the distances can be up to 50km.

Robert Heffernan was one of the best in the world at race walking. People in Cork often saw him training on the roads around the city. He was disqualified from the 2004 Olympics race but in 2012 he did brilliantly to finish fourth, just outside the medals. However, Heffernan was later awarded the bronze medal when a Russian athlete was suspended. Heffernan became a world champion in 2013, capping a brilliant career of putting one foot in front of the other for his country.

IRELAND'S BOBSLEIGH TEAM

Ireland usually sends a small team to the Winter Olympics, but we've had some highlights. Bobsleigh is a really technical, fast and dangerous sport. A team pushes a sleigh down a track to reach speeds of about 40km/h before they jump in! Once they're all inside a pilot steers it through twists and turns in a high speed race against the clock. We don't have much of a tradition of it in Ireland.

A businessman named Larry Tracey set about creating a team in the 1980s, however. He recruited Olympic rowers and other athletes, taught them how to bobsleigh and they did enough to make it to the 1988 Olympics in Calgary, Canada. However their entry was withdrawn because some officials thought we'd be embarrassed and the team couldn't go, sadly. Four years later, though, two two-man teams made it to Albertville in France for the Olympics and they performed admirably, justifying their place at the Winter Games.

THE PARALYMPICS

The Paralympic Games are a major sports competition for athletes with a range of disabilities. The Paralympics take place just after the Olympics every four years, in the same host city. Paralympic athletes compete in six different disability categories: amputee, visual impairment, cerebral palsy, intellectual disability, wheelchair and 'others'. In each group athletes are split into classes based on their disability.

Sports for athletes with disabilities became more organised and widespread after World War II. The Paralympics developed after Sir Ludwig Guttman organised a sports competition for British war veterans with spinal cord injuries in England in 1948. More competitions followed as experts realised how powerful sport was in people's recovery. The first Paralympic Games took place in Rome in 1960 and it's grown in scale and popularity since.

The word 'Paralympic' derives from the Greek preposition *para* – which means beside or alongside – and the word Olympic, which comes from *Olumpikos*, which means 'of Olympia'.

ELLEN KEANE

Ellen Keane is one of our best-ever swimmers. She was born without the lower part of her left arm and, when she was younger, she tried to hide her arm and worried what people thought. When her father brought her to a swimming meet, she won lots of medals and fell in love with the sport. Keane nearly missed the 2008 Paralympics when her appendix burst, but she made it back and became Ireland's youngest-ever Paralympian at just 13 years of age! She went on to win a bronze medal in the 100m breaststroke in Rio in 2016 and then, amazingly, claimed gold in the 100m breaststroke in Tokyo. She no longer feels the need to hide her arm and tries to be a role model for kids, especially those with disabilities.

MARK ROHAN

Mark Rohan was an under-21 footballer with Westmeath when he had an accident on his motorbike at the age of 20. He was lucky to survive and was left paralysed from his chest down. A decade later he had worked to become a champion in a new sport – hand cycling – that became a major part of his life. In his new sport, his bravery and upper-body strength were big advantages and he became a double gold medallist at the 2012 Games in London.

MICHAEL MCKILLOP

One of the greatest Paralympians of all time, McKillop won an amazing 10 medals at major championships. He represented Ireland at Paralympic Games in Beijing, London and Rio, winning four gold medals.

McKillop has a mild form of cerebral palsy that affects his right side. After the London Games, he was given a special award to go with his two gold medals – for demonstrating the best spirit of the Games.

KATIE-GEORGE DUNLEVY

When Katie-George Dunlevy was diagnosed with a rare eye condition at just 11 years of age her life changed completely. As her vision deteriorated, she eventually couldn't see any more and found it very difficult to deal with the change. When she found sport, however, it helped her feel better about herself. She first took on rowing, and became incredibly good. She was then asked to try Paralympic tandem cycling – where two cyclists race on one bike! Dunleavy was paired with Eve McCrystal, who can see and who acts as the sighted pilot for the duo in their races. The pair were soon making a big impact on the track, and have gone on to win medals at multiple games, including gold in Tokyo.

JASON SMYTH

Jason Smyth is one of our most successful athletes ever and was acclaimed as 'the fastest Paralympic runner on the planet'. The Derry native, who has less than 10% vision due to an eye condition, competed at four paralympic Games. Amazingly, he never lost a competitive Para-athletics event throughout his entire career. He won gold medals in every event in which he competed, including six medals at the Paralympic Games in the 100m and 200m events. He also competed in non-Paralympic athletics.

OLYMPIC AQUATICS & THE SPECIAL OLYMPICS

THE SKIBBEREEN ROWERS

Gary and Paul O'Donovan stunned the sports world at the 2016 Rio Olympics by winning Ireland's first-ever rowing medal – a silver – at the Games. And they made their route to success sound so simple. 'Close your eyes and just pull like a dog,' they told people. Their funny interviews and amazing performances made them big stars, and soon the O'Donovans were sitting next to movie actors on the *Graham Norton Show*. The brothers are members of the Skibbereen Rowing Club in West Cork. Although it's a town of only 2,000 people, 'Skibb' has an incredible record of producing world-class rowers.

Four years later in Tokyo, Paul was joined in the boat by another one, Fintan McCarthy, and the pair went one better than in Rio to seal gold with dominant performances on the water.

Want to be a top-class rower? 'You just kind of pull on the oars and race other people,' Paul says.

SANITA PUŠPURE

Originally from Latvia, Sanita Pušpure moved to Ireland in 2006 and has represented Ireland at three Olympic Games. She only took up rowing in Ireland as a hobby after her daughter was born but quickly became one of our top athletes. Puspure was back-to-back world champion in 2018 and 2019 and has won European titles.

MICHELLE SMITH DE BRUIN

Michelle Smith (later known by her married name de Bruin) burst onto the world stage when she won three gold medals and a bronze in the pool at the Atlanta Olympic Games in 1996. Born in Dubin in 1969, Smith was a talented underage swimmer and went to the USA for college, where she competed. She qualified for the 1988 and 1992 Olympics but made no real impact. In 1994 Smith moved to the Netherlands with her coach and future husband, Erik de Bruin, to prepare for the 1996 Games.

In one week in Atlanta, Smith rewrote the history books as she became the first Irishwoman to claim gold at the Games and became our most successful Olympian.

Smith's improvement was so sudden that many athletes and journalists questioned if it had been achieved fairly. Some people suggested she had cheated by taking drugs. Smith denied these allegations and insisted she had competed fairly. A couple of years later, however, Smith received a four-year ban for tampering with a urine sample during a drug test. She has never been stripped of her Olympic medals.

ANNALISE MURPHY

Annalise Murphy grew up dreaming of competing in sailing at the Olympics like her mother did. She'd try on the 1988 Ireland team uniform after practising all day. She eventually made it to the Games in London in 2012, but it ended in disappointment. After looking certain to claim a medal, she ended up finishing fourth to miss out narrowly. She was really disappointed afterwards but promised to be back. When she went to Rio four years later, she performed brilliantly to claim a silver medal for Ireland.

SPECIAL OLYMPICS

The Special Olympics is the world's biggest sports organisation for people with an intellectual disability. The Special Olympic Games are a huge event now but they had humble beginnings.

Eunice Kennedy – the sister of the American president John F. Kennedy – held a summer day camp for children with intellectual disabilities in her backyard in 1962. The event was a big success and the camps spread through North America, growing in popularity until they became the Special Olympics, the first of which took place in Chicago in 1968. Today, millions of athletes take part in Special Olympics qualifying events around the world, while the Olympics themselves take place every two years.

Ireland welcomed the Games in 2003 with an amazing opening ceremony at Croke Park. It was the first time the Games were held outside the United States, and it was the largest sporting event on the planet that year.

GREAT OLYMPIC MOMENTS

JOHN PIUS BOLAND

Though not yet an independent nation, the first Irish-born winner of an Olympic gold medal was John Pius Boland. The Dubliner won the tennis singles event in Athens in 1896 and even won our second Olympic gold medal when he partnered Fritz Traun in the doubles.

Boland went along to the Games to witness the action after a semester of study in Germany. After a party in Athens he decided to give the Olympic tennis event a go.

He borrowed clothes and a racket but went on to win the event.

For many years, Boland's wins were credited to Great Britain, but after a lot of work by academics, his medals are now Irish.

JOHN TREACY

The much-loved TV sports commentator Jimmy Magee listed all Ireland's previous Olympic medal winners as John Treacy ran for the line and second place in Los Angeles in 1984.

The Waterford man is one of our greatest ever long-distance runners and was known for his tenacity, a quality that defined his greatest ever result: a silver medal in the marathon at the 1984 Olympics in Los Angeles. Well down the field for the first half of the race, Treacy entered the top six around the 20km mark, then continued to make great progress until eventually storming into the famous Los Angeles Coliseum stadium just behind second-placed British athlete Charlie Spedding. With the crowd roaring him on, Tracy kicked past Spedding with only 150m to go.

PETER O'CONNOR

Peter O'Connor was one of three athletes in 1906 who raised money themselves to get to the Olympics. They were adamant they wanted to represent Ireland. The Olympics officials denied the request, though, and they were listed as British participants. O'Connor finished second in the long jump competition, securing silver and a place on the podium. When Britain's union flag was raised at the medal presentation, O'Connor shinned up the flagpole and replaced it with a large green flag emblazoned with the words: Erin go Bragh.

BOB TISDALL

Robert Morton Newburgh Tisdall – or just, Bob – was born in Ceylon, or Sri Lanka as it is now, in 1907. Irish by heritage – his father won the All-Irish Sprint Championship and his mother played hockey for Ireland – he wrote a letter to General Eoin O'Duffy, who was then president of the Irish Olympic Council. Tisdall asked to be considered for the Irish Olympic Team in the 400m hurdles, though he admitted he'd never run in the event. O'Duffy invited the young athlete to Croke Park for trials. Tisdall failed to make the time but was given another shot and made the team by winning the 440-yard hurdles.

At the Olympics, Tisdall made it to the final, where he stumbled at the very first hurdle. Despite this bad start he stormed to gold. His time of 51.7 seconds would have been a world record but for the fact that he had knocked over the last hurdle – the rule was changed soon afterwards. He was glad he'd asked for a chance to represent Ireland.

MELBOURNE – 5 IRISH MEDALS

The Melbourne Games in 1956 were hugely successful for the Irish team. Ronnie Delany won a gold medal for Ireland in the 1,500m in the highlight. But along with Delany's gold, Dublin boxer Fred Tiedt earned silver in the welterweight division. As well as that, fellow boxers John Caldwell, Fred Gilroy and Anthony Byrne all won bronze medals in their respective flyweight, bantamweight and lightweight divisions. The Irish team made the long journey home with an unprecedented five medals.

TOM KIELY

Tom Kiely could argue he's Ireland's greatest ever athlete. He won over 50 national titles, two world titles and an Olympic gold medal in the 'all-around', which later became the decathlon. He set numerous world records along the way and earned the nickname 'The Champion Kiely'.

Kiely paid his own way to America in 1904 for the Games in St Louis. The all-around took place on 4 July in heavy rain, which suited the Tipperary man. The 10 disciplines comprised the 100 yards, shot-put, high jump, 880-yard walk, hammer, pole vault, 120-yard high hurdles, 56lb-weight throw, long jump and mile run. Kiely, wearing a shamrock on his vest, claimed gold. He wrote a postcard to his family afterwards which began: 'Well, I won the world championship'.

CYCLING

Countries like France and Belgium are the traditional powerhouses of professional cycling but Ireland has made a massive impact in the sport. We've had a long and intense love affair with cycling and have exported some of cycling's biggest stars over the years.

DID YOU KNOW?
The Tour de France Femmes for female cyclists was launched in 2022. Over the years, several races were held as a Tour de France equivalent for women, with the first in 1955. These races often failed due to lack of support and financial difficulties. Some top female professionals pushed for the Tour de France Femmes, however, which has been a big success.

TOUR DE FRANCE JERSEYS

The Tour is the most prestigious race and takes place over three weeks each summer. Different jerseys are handed out each day to mark different achievements.

YELLOW JERSEY: worn by the overall leader, the person with the best time. It is the most prized jersey.

POLKA-DOT JERSEY: also known as the 'King of the Mountains' jersey, is worn by the best 'climber' in the mountains.

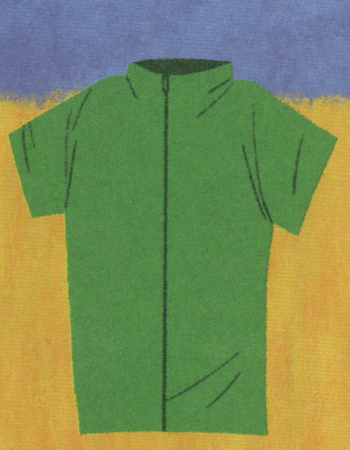

GREEN JERSEY: awarded to the best sprinter in the *peloton*, the pack of riders.

WHITE JERSEY: awarded to the best young rider – under 25 years of age – in the 'general classification'.

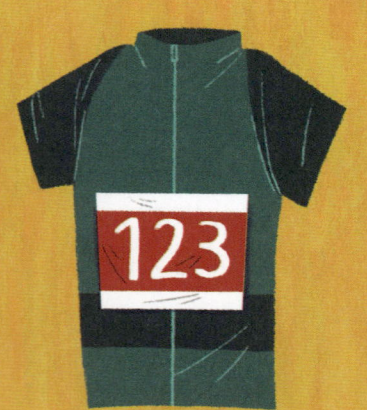

WHITE ON RED NUMBER: awarded to the rider with the most 'fighting spirit'.

SHAY ELLIOTT

Elliott led the way for Irish cycling – but he didn't ride a bike until he was 14 or 15.

He became the top amateur and turned professional in 1957 – something that was highly unusually for an English-speaking cyclist then. He pedalled his way into the history books by becoming the first rider from Britain and Ireland to wear the famous yellow jersey at the Tour de France. He competed in the race five times as well as earning a podium finish at the Vuelta a España. Elliot died tragically at the age of 36, and though his achievements on the continent didn't earn him the recognition they deserved at home, he is now a hero for Ireland's cycling community. The Shay Elliott memorial race takes place every year and passes a memorial that commemorates the Wicklow native.

ROCHE'S TOUR DE FRANCE

Stephen Roche's Tour de France victory was very dramatic and one of the event's standout moments in its century-long history. In second place entering the high mountains in the Alps, his rival Pedro Delgado opened up a big lead. But Roche gritted his teeth and counter-attacked to close the gap to four seconds at the end of the stage. It was a superhuman effort that earned him the yellow jersey but he collapsed and had to spend the night in hospital. However, he recovered enough to get back on his bike and keep the leader's jersey all the way to Paris.

SEAN KELLY

We may not have royalty in Ireland anymore but we have 'King Kelly'. The Carrick-on-Suir man was one of the best and most consistent road racers of his generation. When world rankings were introduced in 1984, he was the first No. 1 and held the top spot for five years. He was known for being tough and determined and won many one-day races, including seven consecutive editions of the prestigious Paris–Nice, and the Vuelta a España – Spain's version of the Tour de France. He was part of the golden generation of Irish riders in the 1980s along with Stephen Roche, Paul Kimmage and Martin Earley and is one of the great 'Classics' stars.

STEPHEN ROCHE

Only one other rider – cycling's greatest, Eddy Merckx – had a year that compares to Stephen Roche's achievements in 1987. The Dubliner left his job as a fitter to try and make it cycling in France. 'People said I'd get as far as the Eiffel Tower. Go round it once and come home again,' he once said. Roche turned professional in 1981 and worked hard to establish himself. In '87, he became a global star by claiming the winner's pink jersey at the Giro d'Italia before going on to win the Tour de France. A quarter of a million people welcomed him home and a few weeks later he won the World Championships in Austria, meaning he could wear the famous rainbow jersey for a year. Only 'The Cannibal' Merckx had done cycling's Triple Crown before and no one has achieved it since.

DID YOU KNOW?

Roche's son Nicolas went on to have an excellent professional cycling career and his nephew Dan Martin followed in his uncle's slipstream by winning two stages at the Tour de France.

SPORTING PIONEERS

TRAILBLAZERS

Ireland has always produced sportspeople who have pushed boundaries, broken barriers and blazed a trail for the rest of us who come after them.

ZAK MORADI

Zak Moradi fled the Iran–Iraq war in the 1980s with his family. They made their home in Leitrim, where Zak soon found himself playing the new game of hurling. He went on to represent his county, and win with them, in Croke Park.

CHRIS HUGHTON

Chris Hughton was a stylish and reliable full back for Spurs. His grandmother from Limerick visited his family every summer. When the East London native was offered the chance to play for his mother's country, he jumped at the opportunity, and he pulled on the green jersey for his debut in a friendly against the USA at Dalymount Park in 1979. That appearance also made Hughton the first black player to play for the Republic of Ireland. He went on to win 53 caps for the team and later was Brian Kerr's assistant manager.

FRANCIE BARRETT

Francie Barrett was a talented southpaw boxer from Galway. He was also the first Traveller to represent Ireland at the Olympics. Barrett was given the honour of carrying the tricolour and leading the Irish athletes into the opening ceremony in Atlanta in 1996.

He got there despite not having many opportunities or even fancy training facilities. Because he didn't have a local boxing club, he made the best of the situation and trained with his coach, Chick Gillen, in a shipping container in Galway.

Barrett won brilliantly in his first fight but lost his second and his Olympic dream was over. He was welcomed back to Galway as a national hero, however, and he'd broken down a barrier for his community along the way.

DONAL ÓG CUSACK

The Cork goalkeeper won three All-Ireland hurling medals and changed the way the game is played with his short puck-out strategy, which took skill and lots of bravery. He also became the first openly gay inter-county GAA player when he told people in 2009.

LENA RICE

Lena Rice is the only Irishwoman to ever win the Wimbledon singles tennis championship – and she only played a handful of tournaments in a short career.

Rice was born into a Big House in 1866, in New Inn in south Tipperary. She played tennis with her sister Anne and her local club in Cahir. By 1889 she'd qualified for Wimbledon – even then the most prestigious tennis tournament in the world – but lost in the final. The next year she went one better and took the title – though there were only four entries.

The Victorian-era Irishwoman from Tipp is credited with inventing the overhead smash that players still use to win majors to this day. Rice sadly died too young, on her 41st birthday, due to tuberculosis.

DANNO O'MAHONY

Danno O'Mahony was the equivalent of Hulk Hogan or The Rock, a household name and world champion wrestler. As a child he was known for his strength, and before long his wrestling skills were spotted. He was brought to America where the sport was hugely popular. He developed the 'the Irish Whip' as his move – where an opponent is spun by the arms into the ropes or a turnbuckle – and earned a shot at the title in 1935 by beating fellow contenders like 'Jumping' Joe Savoldi, Chief Little Wolf and King Clancy.

The 22-year-old Irishman took on the champion Ed Don George and beat him, controversially. A riot broke out, but O'Mahony was declared the champion in front of 60,000 spectators in Boston. He was welcomed back with the belt to Ballydehob, where the local people lit bonfires and filled the streets with music. A lifesize bronze statue of O'Mahony, posing in a wrestling ring, proudly stands in the town, which you can visit.

MAEVE KYLE

When Maeve Shankey became Ireland's first female track Olympian, she faced a lot of criticism and not much support – in 1958, lots of people in Ireland thought women shouldn't compete in top level sport.

Kyle was a talented sportsperson, though, growing up in Kilkenny where she regularly beat her brothers and other boys in games and races.

She studied at Trinity College in Dublin and became an Irish hockey international. When she met the man who would become her husband, Sean Kyle, he encouraged her to try running and he became her coach. After lots of hard work, she managed to earn a place at the Olympics in Melbourne.

She was determined to get there and show the people of Ireland what she was capable of. She proudly represented Ireland at the Games and made history by wearing the Irish singlet on the Olympic track. And she led the way for athletes like Sonia O'Sullivan and Ciara Mageean in later years.

RISING STARS

So who'll write the next chapter in Ireland's sporting story? We've learned about sporting legends, trailblazers and superstars, but as Christy Ring once said, 'the best hurlers are with us now and better yet to come'. The next generation of players and athletes will continue our sporting tradition and amaze us with their accomplishments. Here are just some of the young stars we should keep an eye on.

RHASIDAT ADELEKE

Rhasidat Adeleke is the quickest Irishwoman ever! She's broken Irish records at 60m, 100m, 200m and 400m and won RTÉ's Young Sportsperson of the Year in 2022. And she's just getting started.

Adeleke is of Nigerian descent and is considered one of the brightest prospects in Irish athletics. She played lots of sports growing up, with her mother Ade driving her to races, training sessions and matches.

After school she went to the University of Texas, where she's the first Irishwoman to win a National Collegiate Athletics Association sprint title.

In 2023, Adeleke decided to go professional and signed a big sponsorship deal with Nike.

OISÍN O'CALLAGHAN

Oisín O'Callaghan has been riding bikes since he was three years of age. When he was just seven he told his teacher he wanted to be a world champion mountain-bike rider.

In 2020, he won the famous rainbow jersey by winning the Downhill Mountain Bike Junior Championships in Austria, hitting speeds of over 60km/h.

Mountain-bike racing is really fast and bumpy but Oisín developed his amazing skill racing around the Ballyhoura mountains near his home in Ardpatrick.

RÓISÍN NÍ RÍAIN

At just 16 years of age, Róisín was the youngest competitor at the entire Tokyo Paralympics. The Limerick swimmer did brilliantly, getting to five finals and recording four personal bests – her fastest races ever.

NHAT NGUYEN

Nhat Nguyen was born in Vietnam, coming to Ireland with his parents when he was six years old. After moving, badminton helped him settle into his new country. He followed his dad to the local club and soon fell in love with the game. He became U-17 European champion and practised a lot while he was in school.

Nhat represented Ireland at the Olympics in Tokyo and hopes to be in the green jersey in Paris too.

ADAM SCREENEY

Adam Screeney follows a rich tradition of skilful and entertaining hurlers from Offaly. The Kilcormac-Killoughey forward scored 5-51 across the 2022 minor championship, driving the Faithful County to the decider. Offaly lost out to neighbours Tipperary but Screeney was named player of the championship. The following year he again inspired Offaly to an All-Ireland decider, against Cork at U20 level. It won't be long before Screeney is lighting up the senior game.

RISING STARS

BEIBHINN PARSONS

Beibhinn Parsons burst onto the scene with Ireland's senior women's rugby team as a 16-year-old, scoring a try in her first game against Scotland. She missed some games early on in her career because of her dedication to school, and she's now a key part of Ireland's seven-a-side team, and the 15s game.

EVAN FERGUSON

Evan Ferguson is the most exciting young Irish soccer player to come along in ages. From Bettystown in Co. Meath, he's already scored for Ireland and established himself as a Premier League player with Brighton and Hove Albion. And he's still just a teenager!

Even though he's young, Evan is a tall, strong striker with an excellent touch, thanks to lots of practice. His dad was a professional soccer player too so maybe he got some hints along the way.

Before going to England, Evan played for Bohemians in the League of Ireland. Amazingly, he made his debut for the senior team in a friendly against the mighty Chelsea at just 14 years of age.

ISRAEL OLATUNDE

Israel Olatunde is the fastest Irishman ever and part of a new generation of sprinters in green singlets. He became the first Irishman to appear in the 100m final at the European championships and clocked a national record 10.17 to finish sixth.

AARON HILL

Aaron Hill is a snooker player from Cork. When he was just 18 he beat the best player to ever cue it up, Ronnie 'The Rocket' O'Sullivan. 'To play my childhood hero, live on TV, and then to beat him was just a dream come true,' he said afterwards. He promises it's not a one-off, however.

DAVID CLIFFORD

David Clifford is a GAA superhero. The Kerry forward can do anything with a ball and might just be pushing his way into the association's Hall of Fame. And he's still only 24. The Gaelic football world first took notice of the Fossa youngster during his two years at minor when he won two All-Irelands. He scored four goals and four points in the 2017 final as captain. Since turning senior he's led the Kerry team from the front, helping them to end a wait for Sam Maguire in 2022, while winning thousands of fans all over the country.

MONA MCSHARRY

Mona McSharry is one of the best swimmers we have. Her best event is the breaststroke, but she broke records in four different events while she was still a teenager. Not only that, Mona and her family won Ireland's Fittest Family in 2019. What can't she do!

A HISTORY OF GOLF IN IRELAND

Golf, as an organised game, originated on the east coast of Scotland. Players would try to strike a pebble through sand dunes with a stick, and the first golf courses were fields that sheep had grazed on. The game grew in popularity and various British kings and queens gave the sport its seal of approval.

During the 19th century, as the British empire expanded, golf was exported around the globe. The first golf club formed outside Scotland was the Royal Blackheath near London in 1766, before Royal Curragh in Kildare was established in Ireland in 1856 (records even show a match was played there in 1852). Since then, Ireland has been obsessed with the game, and we're known throughout the world for our amazing courses and our players who have won the biggest competitions.

THE GAME

A round of golf is usually played over 18 holes. The player who gets the ball into the holes in the fewest shots wins. Simple, right? Courses have various obstacles like bunkers of sand, water and areas of longer grass. Each hole has a par score – this is the number of shots you're expected to take to get the ball in. So, if you take one more shot than par, you go one over.

TYPES OF CLUBS

Golfers use a variety of clubs to strike the ball. Each club has a special job – a driver with a large clubhead is used to lash the ball off the tee, while a putter is taken from the bag when a golfer wants to tap the ball into the hole.

OUR BEST GOLF COURSES

Ireland is known the world over for our challenging and beautiful golf courses – especially traditional 'links' courses, which are located along the coast and have sandy soil underfoot. Some of our most well-known courses are Waterville in Kerry, Lahinch in Clare and Portmarnock in Dublin.

PHILOMENA GARVEY

Born in the village of Baltray in Co. Louth, Garvey learned to play on the local course. Working in Clery's department store in Dublin, she was allowed time off to return home to practice. She chose not to marry, since in those days it would mean she would have to give up her true love, golf.

An accomplished amateur golfer, Philomena won the Ladies British Open Amateur Championship in 1957. But she's perhaps best known for a principled stand that cost her a chance at one of her sport's biggest prizes. The best ladies golfer in Ireland, she represented Britain and Ireland in the Curtis Cup against the US six times. However, when the organisers produced a new emblem for the team which was made up of the Union Jack flag, Garvey refused to play if there was no recognition of Ireland. Another badge was adopted two years later, but, although she felt able to play, she was not selected for the team again. Garvey died of a heart attack at Baltray golf club in 2009, at age 83.

CHRISTY O'CONNOR SR

Before the modern wave of successful Irish golfers, O'Connor was considered our greatest golfer ever. The Dubliner was known for a beautiful, smooth swing and for a time was the best player in Britain and Ireland. He was a Ryder Cup star and appeared a then record number of times. His nephew Christy Jr went on to become an important player in the tournament too.

DID YOU KNOW?

Today's golf balls are made from hard rubber and plastic and are scientifically engineered with aerodynamic dimples. In the past, golfers played with wooden balls. They were replaced in the 1600s by boiled feathers stuffed in a leather cover. Later people started making balls with gutta-percha, a leathery material that comes from certain trees. Fore!

MARY HEZLET

Mary Hezlet is arguably our greatest ever female golfer, and a brilliant sportswriter. She was born in Gibraltar but grew up in Co. Derry as part of a well-known golfing family. She started playing at age nine and became the youngest winner of the British amateur championship at 17. Her regular routine of cycling almost 20 miles to Portrush to play 36 holes helped her outlast her opponents.

She went on to win a three-in-a-row of Irish championship victories between 1904 and 1906, and defeated her sister Florence in three Irish finals over the course of their careers. She retired from golf after marrying, but went on to write lots of books and articles about the sport like *Ladies Golf* which was very popular and instructed women on how to take up the game and improve.

THE MODERN GOLF BALL

BEST IRISH GOLFERS

THE MAJORS

Golf has four major tournaments that are played each year.

THE MASTERS
is played at the same course, Augusta National in Georgia in the US, every April. The winner doesn't get a trophy; they get a special green jacket.

THE OPEN
was first played in 1860 and is the oldest golf tournament in the world.

THE US OPEN AND THE US PGA
are played in different venues each year in the states.

DID YOU KNOW?
A golf ball hit by one of the world's strongest players, like Rory McIlroy, can reach speeds of over 180mph!

PÁDRAIG HARRINGTON
Known as one of the hardest workers in golf, Pádraig Harrington won three major championships in just over a year, starting in 2007, when he won the Open at Carnoustie in Scotland after lots of near misses. It made him the first Irish golfer since Fred Daly in 1947 to win a major and the first golfer ever from the Republic of Ireland to do it. The following year he defended his Open title and added the PGA Championship in America. He captained the 2021 European Ryder Cup team and was part of four teams as a player. He even represented Ireland at the Olympics when golf made its return to the Games in 2016 in Rio.

FRED DALY
Fred Daly won the Open by a single shot in 1947 to become Ireland's first ever major winner. He was born in Portrush in 1911 and learned to play as a caddie at the famous golf course in the town. He was the first Irish golfer to play for Britain in the Ryder Cup (the team now represents all of Europe). As well as the Open, he won tournaments like the PGA Match Play and led the way for Irish golfers in the professional game.

THE 2006 RYDER CUP

Golf is usually an individual sport but there are team formats too. The Ryder Cup is the top team competition in golf and is played every two years between the USA and Europe. Ireland hosted the tournament in 2006. The K Club saw big stars like Tiger Woods come to Kildare with the American team, but Irish players like Pádraig Harrington, Darren Clarke and Paul McGinley helped the hosts to a famous victory.

THE LINGO

FORE! The warning you shout when you hit a ball in people's direction

EAGLE: two under par

BIRDIE: a score of one less than par

ACE: a hole in one

PAR: the number of strokes expected for you to get the ball in the hole

ALBATROSS: three under par

BOGEY: one over par

SHANE LOWRY

Shane Lowry grew up playing Gaelic football – his father was an All-Ireland winner with Offaly – but he fell in love with golf and was a brilliant talent. He burst onto the scene by winning the Irish Open. But because he was still an amateur he couldn't keep the prize money. That was the first of two amazing home victories for Shane. In 2019, he made history by winning the first Open championship to be held in Ireland for over 68 years!

RORY MCILROY

When Rory McIlroy made his first television appearance at the age of nine, chipping golf balls into a washing machine, he was already one of the best young players in the world. As he grew older, he excelled at every level, and by the age of 23 he had already won two majors. He's won four to date, more than any other Irish player, and has spent over 100 weeks as the No. 1 ranked golfer. He grew up in Holywood, Co. Down but lives in the US now, where he plays most of his tournaments.

LEONA MAGUIRE

Leona and her twin sister Lisa did everything together. When Lisa injured her arm, they took up golf together to help Lisa recover. They got really good at it and won loads of tournaments as they grew up in Cavan. They earned scholarships to the US to study and play the game there and Leona was the top ranked amateur in the world. Leona turned professional and is the first Irishwoman to win on the prestigious LPGA Tour.

SNOOKER AND DARTS

SNOOKER

Snooker is a really skilful indoor game for two players. It's played on a large table covered in a smooth green felt material called a baize.

Players use long, thin sticks called cues to hit a white cue ball at another coloured ball. There are 21 target balls – the 15 red balls are worth one point each and then there's yellow, green, brown, blue, pink and the most valuable black ball.

Each ball has to be potted in sequence and each game is called a frame. At big tournaments like the world championships at the Crucible in Sheffield, the top players have to win up to 18 frames against an opponent to win the match. Ireland has produced world champions and much-loved personalities in the game.

SOME GREAT SNOOKER NICKNAMES

Judd Trump
THE ACE IN THE PACK

Neil Robertson
THE THUNDER FROM DOWN UNDER

Mark Selby
THE JESTER FROM LEICESTER

ALEX HIGGINS

Snooker can be a slow game that rewards concentration, but Alex Higgins earned his nickname because of the way he played. The 'Hurricane' was a fan favourite in the 1970s and 80s. Higgins came from Belfast and was a big character as snooker became more and more popular on TV. He won the world championship in 1972 and then again 10 years later by beating Ray Reardon. A very emotional Higgins holding his baby daughter in one hand and the trophy in the other is one of the most iconic moments in snooker history.

DENNIS TAYLOR

Dennis Taylor was a hugely popular player, known for the special glasses he wore. They were extra big so he could see the whole table when he played a shot. More importantly, he played in and won the most famous game in snooker history – the 1985 world championship final against multi-time champion, Steve Davis. The match came down to the last ball – whoever potted it was world champion! The biggest TV audience for a snooker tie ever – over 18 million people – stayed up past midnight to see Taylor sink the black and then wag his finger at the crowd in celebration.

DID YOU KNOW?

A break in snooker is the score you build up by potting balls in one go. The maximum break is 147 and they're pretty rare. Ronnie O'Sullivan has the record for the fastest 147 ever at five minutes and eight seconds, which he recorded at the Crucible in 1997. No wonder they call him 'The Rocket'.

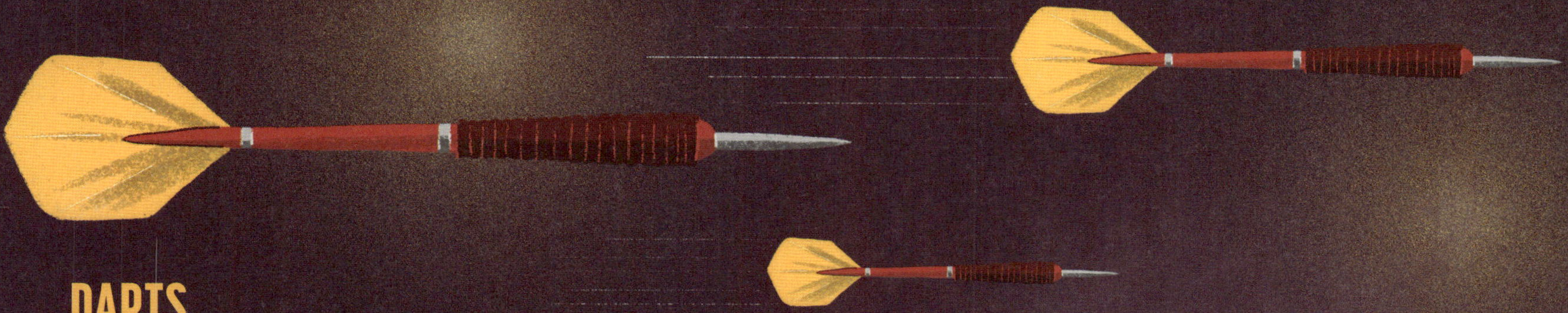

DARTS

Darts is a game where players throw steel arrows at a circular target on a wall, called a dartboard. The dartboard is split into 20 sections and there are two circles in the middle with the very centre called the bullseye. The player must throw their darts from behind a line known as the oche.

The highest score that can be made by throwing three darts in one round is 180. This is where all three darts hit the 'triple 20' section. If you score this, you'll hear the referee shout 'One hundred and eighty!'

Darts is most popular in Britain and is traditionally a pub game, where people have teams and play in tournaments. The PDC world championships are held in the Alexandra Palace – or Ally Pally – in London each year and players from all over Europe and the world compete for the title over the Christmas period.

DID YOU KNOW?

Darts is thought to have first been played around the 1870s. Dartboards were first made out of wood, which was soaked in water the day before a match.

IRISH DARTS PLAYERS

The 2020s look good for Ireland in darts, with a group of players at the top of their game. Fermanagh's Brendan Dolan, Keane Barry of Meath, and Limerick's William O'Connor – who defeated superstar Michael van Gerwen – are among those leading the way for the Irish at the oche.

KEN DOHERTY

'Crafty' Ken Doherty first learned to play in a snooker hall called Jason's, not far from his home in Ranelagh, Dublin. They gave him a biscuit tin to stand on so he could reach the table properly, as he took on anyone who tried to beat the talented kid.

He practised hard and turned professional in 1991. Six years later he reached the final at the famous Crucible Theatre against the best player in the world, Stephen Hendry. Their final was an epic with 'The Darling of Dublin' winning 18-12 to claim his first world title. More than a quarter of a million people lined the streets of the capital to welcome Doherty home. Doherty reached two more world championship finals and remained one of the game's top players for nearly two decades.

THE WIDER WORLD OF SPORT

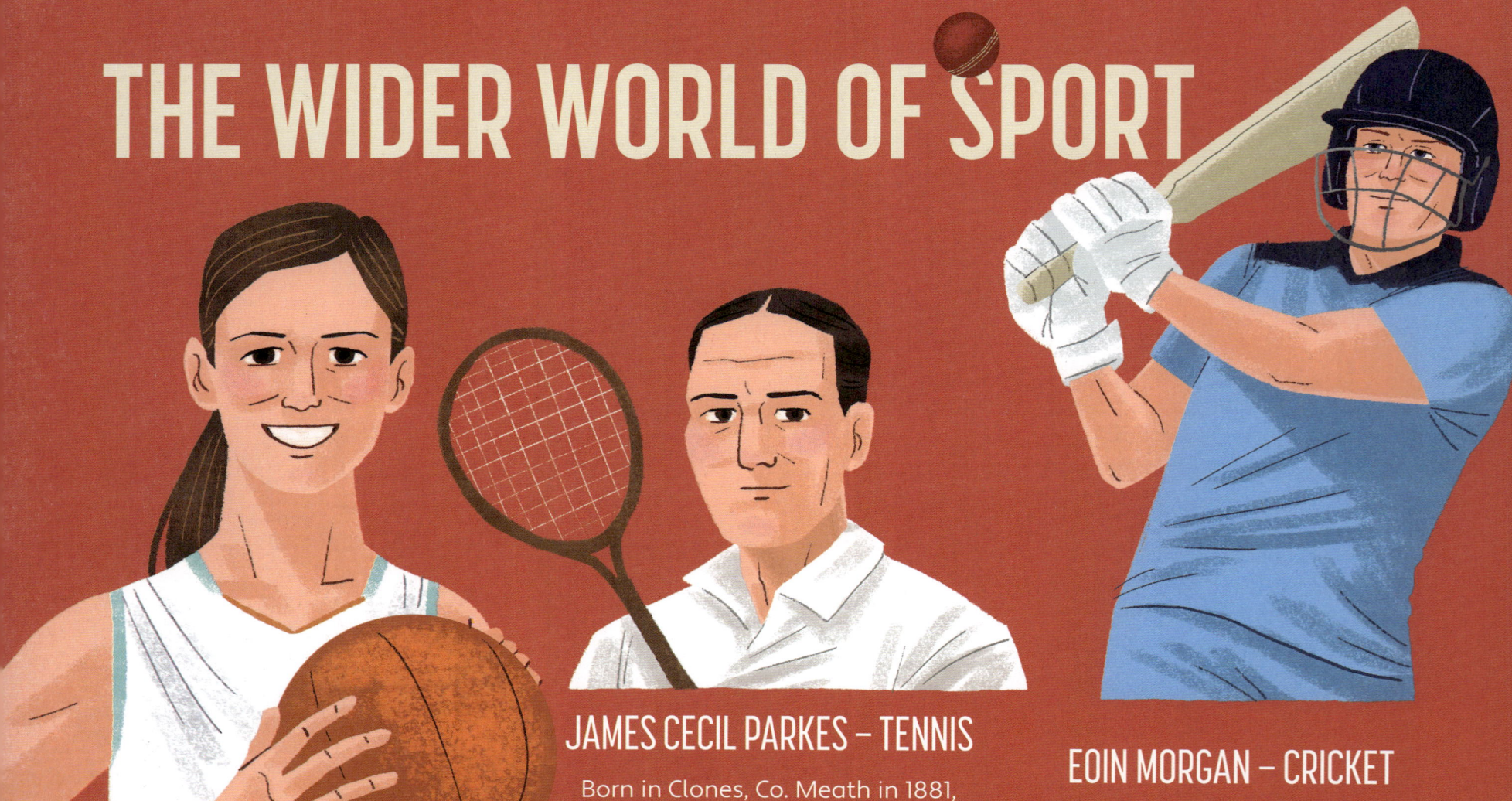

SUSAN MORAN – BASKETBALL

If you're going to make it as a basketball player, America is the place to be. Susan Moran made a huge impact on the hardwood in the states. Moran was a great tennis player but when she tried basketball with her school in Tullamore she led them to a cup double in 1998, breaking scoring records in the finals. She won a scholarship to St Joseph's in Philadelphia, where she was so successful the school retired her jersey after she left and put her in their Hall of Fame. In 2001 she became the first Irishwoman to play in the WNBA when she was drafted by New York Liberty.

JAMES CECIL PARKES – TENNIS

Born in Clones, Co. Meath in 1881, James Cecil Parkes played and excelled at lots of sports but was probably most successful at tennis. He was an Olympic silver medallist (1908), the Australian Open singles and doubles champion in 1912 and a winner at Wimbledon, taking the mixed doubles title in 1914. As well as that, though, he represented Ireland in rugby and golf, was a class cricket player and knew his way around a chess board.

EDDIE MACKEN – SHOWJUMPING

Eddie Macken was Ireland's top showjumper over a 25-year period. He helped the Irish team to the Aga Khan Cup for three years on the trot between 1977 and '79. He was runner-up at the Show Jumping World Championships on a horse named Pele in 1974 and, in 1978, with Boomerang, the horse with whom he was most linked. They won many titles together and when Boomerang died, he was buried at Macken's stud.

EOIN MORGAN – CRICKET

When England won the Cricket World Cup in 2019, they were led there by an Irishman. Eoin Morgan grew up in Rush, in north county Dublin, which has a long cricket tradition. He loved the sport and was part of a generation of Irish players who helped put our country on the map by shocking Pakistan at the World Cup in 2007. Ireland were not a full test nation at the time, however, and when England offered Morgan the chance to play for them, he took it. He was eventually made captain, an especially important job in cricket.

THE TAILTEANN GAMES

In the summer of 1924, Ireland hosted the biggest sporting event in the world that year – bigger even than the Paris Olympics. The Tailteann games – named after an ancient version of the games – saw thousands of competitors take part in sporting events like athletics and swimming, along with competitions for dancing, art and sculpture. The Games were held across Ireland in 1924, '28 and '32. The country had just won independence and the Tailteann Games were seen as a way to establish the new state.

MICK BARRY – ROAD BOWLING

Road bowling is a sport with a long history in Ireland which has a passionate following, particularly in Cork and Armagh. Competitions take place along country roads with competitors attempting to get the 28oz metal ball along the course in the fewest throws possible.

Mick Barry is thought to have been the best bowler ever. He worked as a gardener in University College Cork, but on weekends he competed and won 11 All-Ireland titles in his career. On St Patrick's Day, 1955, in front of 6,000 spectators, he achieved an amazing feat. Barry hurled a 16oz bowl over the 90-foot tall Chetwynd Viaduct in Cork, becoming the first person to do so. He tried later with a 28oz ball but it hit the metalwork at the top. 'The King of the Road' is still regarded as a road-bowling legend.

ROSEMARY SMITH – MOTOR RACING

Rosemary Smyth proved female drivers have all the talent and courage needed to compete and win behind a steering wheel in the male-dominated world of motor racing. Smyth opened a dressmaking shop in Dublin, but when an amateur driver, Delphine Biggar, called into the store one day in 1959, her life changed. She went on to win lots of races, including the famous Tulip Rally in the Netherlands, and undertook epic races across Africa and South America. Once, when her engine broke down in Iran and the car couldn't get over the Khyber Pass in first gear, she reversed up the mountain instead.

THE DUNLOPS – MOTORCYCLING

Motorbike rallying is hugely popular in Northern Ireland. The Dunlops are the most famous family in the sport, and Joey Dunlop is one of the most iconic riders of all. He dominated the famous Isle of Man TT and won many other races. It's a dangerous sport, however, with riders regularly reaching speeds over 120mph, and Joey, his brother Robert and nephew William all died during races.

FUN FACTS

A Premier League team almost relocated to Ireland. A group of businesspeople and media personalities wanted to bring Wimbledon FC here in the 1990s and rename the club the Dublin Dons. There was a lot of opposition to the idea and the club moved to Milton Keynes instead.

Pat Burke is the only Irishman to ever play in the NBA. Burke's family moved from Tullamore in Offaly to Ohio when he was three years old. He grew up – and grew and grew – to be a pro basketball player with franchises like the Orlando Magic and the Phoenix Suns between 2002 and 2007.

Underage players in Wicklow set the record for the Gaelic football match played at the highest altitude in 2006. The players lined out in a makeshift pitch at the summit of Lugnaquilla, the country's third-highest mountain. They threw the ball in at 3,041 feet above sea-level.

Denis Irwin scored the first goal at the new Páirc Uí Chaoimh. The Corkman lined out in a star-studded soccer game between Ireland and Celtic legends and Man Utd legends, which was played in tribute to the late Liam Miller.

MMA is one of the fastest growing sports in the world. Ireland has hosted the biggest promotion, the UFC, on a few occasions in Dublin.

Bohemians FC have released lots of special jerseys in recent years, including shirts with a message welcoming refugees to Ireland, one with a picture of reggae star Bob Marley who played a gig at Dalymount Park, and even one reflecting the distinctive material of Dublin Bus seats.

TOP 10 STADIUMS BY CAPACITY IN IRELAND

1.	Croke Park, Dublin	82,300
2.	Aviva Stadium, Dublin	51,700
3.	Semple Stadium, Thurles, Tipperary	45,690
4.	Pairc Ui Chaoimh, Cork	45,000
5.	Gaelic Grounds Páirc na nGael, Limerick	44,023
6.	Fitzgerald Stadium, Killarney, Kerry	38,000
7.	Casement Park, Belfast, Antrim	34,578
8.	St Tiernach's Park, Clones, Monaghan	29,000
9.	Nowlan Park, Kilkenny	27,000
10.	Pearse Stadium, Galway	26,197

Terry Wogan was a famous chat show host and radio presenter in Britain. Amazingly, he held the record for the longest televised golf putt. The Limerick man sunk a 100 ft putt at the Gleneagles golf course in 1981 during a pro-celebrity TV event.

The Late Late Show host Patrick Kielty was the substitute goalkeeper on Down's All-Ireland winning minor football team in 1987. The Mourne men beat Cork with Kielty a goalkeeper on the panel.

According to latest figures, about half of adults in Ireland take part in some form of sport. Three-quarters of kids in primary school play some extra-curricular sport, often more than twice a week!

Cork is the county with the most GAA clubs – it's estimated there are 259 in the Rebel County.

THE BIG QUIZ

1. Irishman Jack Kirwan was the first professional manager of which famous European soccer club?

2. Who put the ball in the English net (at Euro '88)?

3. Which player scored the winning kick for Ireland in the last 16 shootout at Italia '90?

4. How many international goals did record-holder Robbie Keane score for Ireland?

5. Andrew Kerins founded Celtic in 1888. But what was he better known as?

6. Who was the Arsenal star and international captain that led Ireland to the Women's World Cup 2023?

7. What's the name of the award given to the best goal scored each year? Stephanie Roche earned a nomination with one of her efforts.

8. Who became the GAA's first president after it was established in Thurles in 1884? There's a stand named after him at Croke Park.

9. What kind of weather defined the 1939 All-Ireland hurling final?

10. Who's the only man to win senior All-Ireland medals in hurling and football in the same year?

11. From which tree are hurleys traditionally made?

12. Which song from a Disney movie was the anthem of the Irish women's rugby team's at the 2014 World Cup?

13. What song do Munster fans sing to encourage their players to get up and battle?

14. Who became the first Irish province to win the European Cup when they beat Colomiers in 1999?

15. What's the rugby trophy that Ireland and Scotland play for each year? It sounds like it's from *Harry Potter*!

16. What song did organisers play as the Irish national anthem before the first game of the 1987 Rugby World Cup?

17. At which American Football stadium did Ireland finally beat the All Blacks in 2016?

18. At which football stadium did Barry McGuigan win his world boxing title?

19. Michael Carruth won Olympic gold for Ireland in 1992, but what was his job outside the ring?

20. At which Olympic Games was women's boxing introduced for the first time, with Katie Taylor taking a gold medal?

21. What's the name of the English town where the festival, known as horse racing's Olympics, takes place each March?

22. What was the name of the horse that was kidnapped in 1983 and was never recovered?

23. Which Irish woman became the first Irish jockey to win the Aintree Grand National in 2021?

24. What does the Olympic motto *Citius, altius, fortius* mean?

25. Which West Cork town has produced the O'Donovan brothers and lots of other rowing stars?

26. The yellow jersey goes to the person who wins the Tour de France; what jersey does the King of the Mountains get?

27. Which wrestling move is Danno O'Mahony said to have created?

28. Which Dubliner won the Snooker World Championships in 1997?

29. What's the red circle at the centre of a dart board called?

30. Which two teams face off in the Ryder Cup in golf?

WRITE THE STORY OF YOUR SPORTING HERO

ANSWERS

1. Ajax of Amsterdam
2. Ray Houghton
3. David O'Leary
4. 68
5. Brother Walfrid
6. Katie McCabe
7. The Puskas Award
8. Michael Davin
9. Thunder and lightning
10. Teddy McCarthy (Cork 1990)
11. Ash
12. 'Let It Go', from Frozen
13. 'Stand Up And Fight'
14. Ulster
15. The Centenary Quaich
16. 'The Rose of Tralee'
17. Soldier Field, home of the Chicago Bears
18. Loftus Road
19. Soldier
20. London, 2012
21. Cheltenham
22. Shergar
23. Rachael Blackmore
24. Faster, higher, stronger
25. Skibbereen
26. The polka-dot jersey
27. The Irish Whip
28. 'Crafty' Ken Doherty
29. Bullseye!
30. Europe and the USA

INDEX

A

AC Milan 19
Adeleke, Rhasidat 76
　Sportsperson of the Year (2022) 76
Aga Khan Cup 86
Ajax 7
Aki, Bundee 38
Ali, Muhammad (The Greatest) 49
　Muhammad Ali v Alvin Blue Lewis (1973) 49
　Rumble in the Jungle (1974) 49
　Thrilla in Manila (1975) 49
All Blacks 36, 39, 41, 45
　Munster v All Blacks (1978) 39
　Original All Blacks 37
All Stars 17, 28, 29, 30
All-Ireland Camogie Final (1912) 22
All-Ireland Championships (1887) 21
All-Ireland football final (1947) 25
All-Ireland football final (1951) 25
All-Ireland hurling final (1939) 23
All-Ireland hurling final (1994) 33
All-Ireland hurling final (1995) 25, 29, 33
All-Ireland hurling final (1997) 33
Anderson, Henry J. 38
Arsenal 8, 13, 14, 15, 17
Artane Band 25
Artane Indusrial School 25
Ascoli 13
Aston Villa 14, 19
athletics 26, 62–5, 70–1, 76, 78
　Irish world champions 63, 71
Athlone Town FC 19
Athlone Town v AC Milan (1975) 19
Australian Football League 27
Australian Rules football 27
aviator, Lady Mary Heath 61
Aviva Stadium, Dublin 8, 35, 38, 44
　concerts 35
AZ Alkmaar 19

B

badminton 77
Barca 13
Barrett, Francie 74
Barry, Dave 19
Barry, Keane 85
Barry, Mick 87
basketball 86
Bayern Munich 12, 19
Benn, Nigel 50
Best, George 15
Biggar, Delphine 87
Black Ferns 43
Blackmore, Rachel 58, 59
Blanchflower, Danny 9
Bloody Sunday (1920) 24, 34
Bloomfield Park, Blackpool 7
bobsleigh, Ireland's team 65
Bohemians (Bohs) FC 7, 18, 19
Boland, John Pius 61, 70
　Olympic Gold Medal (1896) 61, 70
Bolger, Jim 59
Bonner, Denis 15
Bonner, Packie 10, 15
boxing 48–53, 74
　Hall of Fame 50
　history of boxing in Ireland 48–9
　IABA, foundation of 48
　Ireland's greatest boxing moments 52
　Irish Olympic Medals (1956) 71
　Olympics (1992) 52
　Olympics (2012) 50, 53
　Olympics (2020) 53
　Queensberry rules 48
　WBO Super Middleweight Champion of the World (1995) 53
　weight classes 49
　women's boxing 48, 50, 51, 53
boxing fights
　Barry McGuigan v Eusebio Pedroza (1985) 52
　Michael Carruth v Juan Hernández (1992) 52
　Muhammad Ali v Alvin (Blue) Lewis (1973) 49
　Rumble in the Jungle (1974) 49
　Steve Collins v Chris Eubank (1995) 53
　Thrilla in Manila (1975) 49
Brady, Liam (Chippy) 13, 14
Bray Wanderers FC 19
Rocky the Seagull (mascot) 19
Brehon Laws 23
Brendan Martin Cup 32
Briggs, Niamh 43, 47
Brogan brothers 32
Brother Walfrid 13
Bruff Rugby Football Club 39
Buckley, Rena 28, 32
'Busby Babes' 8
Busby, Matt 8
Byrne, Anthony 71
Byrne, Emma 17
Byrne, Jack 18

C

Caldwell, John 71
Calzaghe, Joe 50
camogie 21, 22, 28, 29
　greatest players 28, 29
　most successful counties 22
　O'Duffy Cup 22
Camogie Association 21
Canavan, Peter 31
Canning, Joe 29
Cantwell, Lynne 43, 45, 47
Carberry, Nina 58, 59
Carruth, Michael 52
　Michael Carruth v Juan Hernández 52
　Olympics (1988) 52
　Olympics (1992) 52
Celtic Crosses (medals) 23
Celtic Football Club 13, 14, 15
Celtic League 39
Champions League 15
Champions League (1999) 12
Champions League (2004) 19
chariot racing 54
Charles II, King 54
Charlton, Bobby 8, 10, 15
Charlton, Jack (Big Jack) 10, 15, 35
Chelsea 7, 15, 78
City and Suburban Sports Grounds 34
Clarke, Darren 83
Clay, Cassius see Ali, Muhammad
Clifford, David 79
Cluxton, Stephen 30, 32
Cobh Ramblers 12, 18, 19
Cody, Brian 28, 33
Coghlan, Eamonn 63

Coghlan, Fiona 43, 45, 46
Coleman, Seamus 18
Collins, Steve (Celtic Warrior) 50
　Steve Collins v Chris Eubank (1995) 53
　WBO Super Middleweight Champion of the World (1995) 53
Commonwealth Games 51
Compromise Rules (International Rules) 27
Connacht Rugby 38
　'Fields of Athenry, The' 38
　The Sportsground, Galway 38
Cooley Peninsula, County Louth 26
Cooper, Colm (The Gooch) 31
Cordoba, Ricardo 51
Cork City FC 18, 19
　Cork City v Bayern Munich (1991) 19
　Corky the Cheetah (mascot) 19
Cork double (1990) 25
　Liam MacCarthy Cup 25
　Sam Maguire Cup 25
Cork Ladies Football 32
Corkery, Briege 28, 32
Corr, Stephen 12
Coulter, Phil, 'Ireland's Call' 40
Cowboy Skills Rodeo (1924) 34
Coyle, Natalya 64
　modern pentathlon 64
　Olympic Games (2012) 64
cricket 86
Cricket World Cup (2019) 86
Croke Park 13, 20, 23, 34
　Bloody Sunday 24
　boxing: Ali v Lewis (1973) 49
　Canal End terraces 34
　concerts 34
　Cowboy Skills Rodeo (1924) 34
　Cusack Stand 20, 34
　Hawkeye technology 23
　Hogan Stand 24, 34
　Leinster v Munster (rugby) (2009) 38
　Museum 34
　Nally End terraces 34
　Six Nations Rugby 41
　Special Olympic Games (2003) 69
Croke, Thomas, Archbishop of Cashel and Emly 34
Crucible Theatre, Sheffield 84, 85
Cruz, Steve 52
Cú Chulainn 20
Cummins, Brendan 26
Cunningham, Ger 26
Cusack, Donal Óg 74
Cusack, Michael 20
cycling 72–3
　Downhill Mountain Bike Junior Championships 76
　Giro d-Italia 73
　Paris-Nice race 73
　Shay Elliott Memorial Race 72
　Tour de France 72, 73
　Tour de France Femmes 72
　Vuelta a España 72, 73

D

Daly, Fred 82
　PGA Match Play 82
　Ryder Cup team 82
D'Arcy, Gordon 38
darts 85

　Crucible Theatre 85
　dartboard 85
　Irish darts players 85
　PDC World Championships 85
Davin, Michael 20
Davin Stand, Croke Park 20
Davis, Steve 84
de Bromhead, Henry 59
de Bruin, Erik 69
de Coubertin, Pierre 60
Deaper, Tom 56
Delaney, J.J. 33
Delany, Ronnie 35
　Olympic Gold Medal (1956) 52, 61, 71
Delgado, Pedro 73
Dempsey, Jack (Nonpareil) 48
Deportivo La Coruña 19
Derry City Football Club 18, 19
Derry GAA 13
Desmond, Christina 51
Dineen, Frank 34
DLR Waves FC 19
Doherty, Ken (Crafty) 85
　World Championships 85
Dolan, Brendan 85
Downey, Angela 29
Downey, Ann 29
Downhill Mountain Bike Junior Championships 76
Doyle, Jack (Gorgeous Gael) 48
Doyle, John 29
Doyle, John (Holycross Hercules) 29
Doyle, Kevin 19
Doyle, Philip (Goose) 45
Dreaper, Tom 56
Duff, Damien 11, 12, 13, 15
Dundalk FC 19
　Europa League (2016–17) 19
Dunlevy, Katie-George 67
Dunlop, Henry Wallace 35
Dunlop, Joey 87
Dunne, Bernard 51
Dunne, Richard 12
Dunphy, Eamon 14

E

Earley, Martin 73
Easter Rising (1916) 7
Elliott, Gordon 59
Elliott, Shay 72
Elsom, Rocky 38
English Premier League 8
Eubank, Chris 50
　Steve Collins v Chris Eubank (1995) 53
Euro 2016 13
Euro '88 8, 10
Europa League (2016–17) 19
European Cup (1967) 13
European Cup (1968) 15
European Cup (1999) 39
European Cup (2009) 38
European Cup (2011) 38
European Cup tie (1958) 8
European ties 19
　Athlone Town v AC Milan (1975) 19
　Cork City v Bayern Munich (1991) 19
Everton Football Club 9, 18

F

Farrell, Andy 41
FC Barcelona 13

Fenton, Brian 32
Ferguson, Alex 12, 15
Ferguson, Evan 78
FIFA 6, 8
Finn Harps 19
First World War 13
Foley, Anthony 41
Football Association of Ireland (FAI) 6, 7, 16
    FAI Cup 14, 18, 47
Football Team of the Millenium and Century 31
Foster, Charles (Pop) 49

G

GAA (Gaelic Athletic Association) 13, 20-1
    All-Ireland football final (1947) in New York 25
    Artane Band 25
    Celtic Crosses (medals) 23
    clubs, number of 25
    Cork double win (1990) 25
    first All-Ireland championships (1887) 21
    founding of 20
    Liam MacCarthy Cup 21
    Limerick, first football champions 21
    Sam Maguire Cup 21
    Thunder and Lightning Final (1939) 23
    Tipperary, first hurling champions 21
    women's games 21
    wrestling 24
    see also Croke Park
Gaelic football 15, 24, 27, 32, 79
    Bloody Sunday (1920) 24
    Brendan Martin Cup 32
    Cork ladies football 32
    Cork LGFA team 32
    Dublin six in a row 32
    greatest Gaelic footballers 30-1
    Kerry Gold 32
    Limerick, first football champions 21
    the Mayo Curse 25
    Sam Maguire Cup 21
    solo runs 25
Gaelic Grounds, Limerick 29
    Mackey Stand 29
Gallaher, David 37
Galway United FC 19
Galwey, Mick 44
Garvey, Philomena 81
Gatland, Warren 44
Gavin, Jim 32
Giles, John 14
Gillen, Chick 74
Gilroy, Fred 71
Gilroy, Pat 32
Giro d'Italia 73
Given, Shay 12
Glen Rovers 22
Gogarty, Deirdre 48, 51
Gogarty, Oliver St John
    'Ode to the Tailteann Games' 61
    Olympic Bronze Medal (1924) 61
Goldrick, Sinéad 27
golf
    the game 80
    golf balls 81
    history of golf in Ireland 80
    Irish golfers 81-3
    Ryder Cup 82, 83
    types of clubs 80
golf courses
    Baltray 80
    Lahinch 80
    Portmarnock 80
    Waterville 80
golf lingo
    ace 83
    albatross 83
    birdie 83
    bogey 83
    eagle 83
    fore 83
    par 83
golf tournaments
    Ryder Cup 81, 82, 83
    The Masters 82
    The Open 82
    The US Open 82
    US PGA 82
Goodison Park, Liverpool 9
Green Glens Arena, Millstreet 53
Griffin, Anne-Marie 48
Guttman, Sir Ludwig 66

H

handball 26, 27
Harrington, Kellie 50, 51, 53
    Olympic Bronze Medal (2020) 53
Harrington, Pádraig 82, 83
    European Ryder Cup Team (2021) 82
    Olympics (2016) 82
    Open at Carnoustie (2007) 82
    PGA Championship 82
Harte, Micky 31
Hawkeye technology 23
Hayes Hotel, Thurles 20, 21
Hayes, John (The Bull) 39
Heath, Lady Mary 61
Heffernan, Robert 63, 65
Heffo's Army 32
Heineken Cup 39
Henderson, Jill 42
Hendry, Stephen 85
Hernández, Juan 52
Hezlet, Mary 81
    three-in-a-row Irish champion (1904-6) 81
Higgins, Alex (Hurricane) 84
    World Championship (1972) 84
Hill, Aaron 79
hockey
    Ireland's women's hockey team 64
    World Cup final 64
Hogan, Michael 24, 34
Home Farm 8
Horgan, Shane 41
horse races
    Aintree Grand National 55, 58, 59
    Aintree Racecourse 55
    Cheltenham Festival 55, 58, 59
    Cheltenham Gold Cup 55, 56, 58
    Irish Grand National 55, 59
    King's Plate races 54
    Melbourne Cup 56
    Prestbury Cup 55
    Prestbury Park 55
horse racing
    handicap 56
    stud farm 56
    the weighing room 57
horse racing in Ireland 54
    chariot racing in Kildare 54
    first steeplechase 55
    flat racing 54
    the 'going' 54
    greatest Irish horses 56
    Irish Grand National 55
    Irish Jockey Club 54
    Irish jockeys 58-9
    jump racing 54, 55
    National Hunt 54
    point-to-point races 54
    steeplechases 55
    Turf Club 54
horse racing lingo 55
    bit 55
    blinkers 55
    bridle 55
    a furlong 55
    noseband 55
    silks 55
horse trainers 56, 57, 59
horses
    Arkle 56
    Blue Loyd 12 64
    Dawn Run 56
    greatest Irish horses 56
    Hurricane Fly 59
    Istabraq 57
    Organisedconfusion 59
    Papillon 58
    Red Rum 57
    Sea the Stars 57
    Shergar 57
    Tiger Roll 59
    Vintage Crop 56
    Waterford Crystal 64
horses, different names for
    colt 57
    filly 57
    gelding 57
    mare 57
    stallion 56, 57
Houghton, Ray 8, 10
Humphreys, David 39
hurling 20, 22, 23, 74, 77
    Brehon Laws 23
    Celtic Crosses (medals) 22
    the Cody Era 33
    greatest players 28-9
    hurl or hurley 23
    hurley makers 26
    Liam MacCarthy Cup 21, 33
    most successful counties 22
    Munster final replay (1944) 22
    the Revolution Years 33
    the sliothar 23
    Thunder and Lightning Final (1939) 22
    Tipperary, first hurling champions 21
    Young Hurler of the Year 29
hurling headgear 27
Hurling Team of the Millenium 29
hurls/hurleys 23, 26

I

Inter Milan 13, 14
International Rules (Compromise Rules) 27
Ireland Women's Rugby Football Union (IWRFU) 42
Ireland's Fittest Family (2019) 79
Irish Athletic Boxing Association (IABA) 48
Irish Champion Athletic Club 35
Irish Civil War 7
Irish Football Association (IFA) 6, 7
Irish football supporters 8
Irish International Rugby 40-1, 44, 45
    'Amhrán n Bhfiann' 40
    Calcutta Cup 40
    Centenary Quaich 40
    Croke Park (2005) 41
    European Cups 46
    first Ireland game (1975) 36
    Five Nations 35, 44
    Grand Slam (2009) 40, 44
    Grand Slam (2018) 45
    International Hall of Fame 47
    Ireland v England (1875) 36
    'Ireland's Call' 40
    Joe Schmidt Era 45
    Millenium Trophy 40
    Player of the Year (2001) 47
    Player of the Year (2018) 46
    'Rose of Tralee, The' 41
    Six Nations 40, 44, 45
    Soldier Field, Chicago (2016) 41, 45
    Triple Crown 40
    Triple Crown (2004) 44
    World Cup 41
    World Cup (1987) 41
    World Cup (1995) 40
Irish International Soccer 8-15
Irish Premier League
    most appearances 12
    top scorers 13
Irish Republican Brotherhood (IRB) 21
Irish Rugby Football Union (IRFU) 35, 36
    Ireland's greatest player 47
Irish Women's Football 15, 16-17
    World Cup finals (2023) 15
Irish Women's Rugby 42-3, 45, 47, 78
    Grand Slam 43
    Grand Slam (2013) 47
    Ireland v Black Ferns (2014) 43
    Rugby World Cup (1998) 42
    Rugby World Cup (2014) 43, 45
    Six Nations (2013) 47
    Women's Rugby World Cup (2014) 45
    Women's Six Nations 42
Irwin, Denis 15
Isle of Man TT 87
Italia '90 8, 10, 15

J

John Paul II, Pope 10
Johnson, Sammy 7
Jones' Road, Drumcondra 21, 34
Jones, Stephen 40
Juventus 12, 13, 14

K

Kahn, Oliver 11
Keane, Ellen 66
    Bronze Medal (2016) 66
    Gold Medal (2020) 66
Keane, Robbie 11, 13, 14
Keane, Roy 11, 12, 14, 18
Kelly, David 35
Kelly, Sean (King Kelly) 73
    Paris-Nice race 73
    Vuelta a España 73
Kelly, Tom (The Champion Kelly) 71
    Olympic Gold Medal (1904) 71
Kennedy, Eunice 69
Kenny, Stephen 8, 19
Kerins, Andrew (Brother Walfrid) 13
Kerr, Brian 15
Kerry, All-Ireland football titles 32
Kerry Football Club 19
Kidney, Declan 40, 44
Kiely, Tom 71
Kimmage, Paul 73
Kingspan Stadium, Belfast 39
Kirwan, Jack 7
Kyle, Jack 47
Kyle, Maeve 75
Kyle, Sean 75

L

LA Galaxy 14
Ladies Football all-time top scorer 30
Ladies Football Association 21
Lam, Pat 38
Lansdowne Road Stadium 8, 18, 35
    the Landsdowne Roar 35
    riot (1995) 35
Lavin, Sean 25
Law, Denis 15
Lazcano, Juan (The Hispanic Causin' Panic) 48
Lazio 17
League of Ireland 6, 12, 18
    best players 18–19
    First Division 18
    Premier Division 18
League of Ireland mascots 19
Lee, Andy 51
Leeds United 10, 14
Leinster Rugby 38, 45, 46
    European Cup (2011) 38
    European Cup stars 38
    RDS/Aviva Stadium 38
Lewis, Alvin (Blue) 49
Liam MacCarthy Cup 21, 23, 25
Limerick, Leo the Lion (mascot) 19
Liverpool 14
Lohan, rian 33
Long, Shane 13
Longford Town Football Club 19
Loughnane, Ger 33
Lowry, Shane 83
    Irish Open 83
Lynch, Jack 22, 23

M

McAlery, John 6
McAnallen, Cormac 27
McAteer, Jason 11
McAuley, Dave (Boy) 51
McAuliffe, Johnny 23
McCabe, Katie 15
Maccabi Tel Aviv 19
McCain, Ginger 57
MacCarthy, Liam 21
McCarthy, Mick (Captain Fantastic) 11
McCarthy, Teddy 25
    two All-Ireland medals (1990) 25
McCarthy-O'Brien, Jackie 43
McCoy, Anthony (AP) 58
McCrystal, Eve 67
McCullough, Wayne (Pocket Rocket) 51
MacCumhaill, Fionn 54
McDonald, Ciarán 31
McFerrin, Ayesha 64
McGinley, Paul 83
McGrath, Paul 14, 19
McGuigan, Barry (The Clones Cyclone) 48, 51
    Barry McGuigan v Eusebio Pedroza (1985) 52
McIlroy, Rory 82, 83
Macken, Eddie 86
    Aga Khan Cup 86
    Boomerang (horse) (1978) 86
    Pele (horse) (1974) 86
    Show Jumping World Championships 86
Mackey, Mick 29
McKillop, Michael 67
McLarnin, Jimmy (Babyface Assassin) 49
McLoughlin, James (sculptor) 62
McMahon, Philly 32
McMahon, Seanie 29
McManus, J.P. 57
McSharry, Mona 79
Madison Square Garden, New York 49
Magee, Jimmy 70
Mageean, Ciara 63
Maguire, Leona 83
    LPGA Tour 83
Maguire, Sam 21
Manchester City FC 8, 18
Manchester United FC 11, 12, 13, 14, 15, 19
Mancini, Ray (Boom Boom) 48
Martin, Dan 73
mascots, League of Ireland 19
Medal of the Order of Australia (OAM) 27
Melbourne Football Club 27
    Brownlow medal 27
Merckx, Eddy 73
Mills-Hill, Kathleen (Kay) 28
Monaghan, John (Rinty) 51
Moradi, Zak 74
Moran, Susan 86
Morgan, Eddie 86
    Cricket World Cup (2019) 86
motor racing 87
motorcycling
    Dunlop family 87
    Isle of Man TT 87
Motson, John 11
Mourinho, José 15
Mulcahy, Valerie 32
Mullan, Katie 64
Mullins, Paddy 56
Mullins, Willie 59
Munich air disaste (1966) 8
Munster final replay (1944) 22
Munster Rugby 39, 46, 47
    Munster v All Blacks (1978) 39
    Musgrave Park, Cork 39
    'Stand up and Fight' 39
    Thomond Park, Limerick 39
Murphy, Annaliese 69
    Olympic Silver Medal (2016) 69
Murphy, Juliet 32

N

National Stadium, Dublin 48
National Stud, Kildare 56
N'Do, Joey 19
Neville, Joy 43
New Zealand 45
    All Blacks 36, 39, 41, 45
    Black Ferns 43
    Dave Gallaher Trophy 37
    Original All Blacks 37
    White Ferns 45
Nguyen, Nhat 77
    U-17 European Champion 77
Ní Chinnéide, Máire 21
Ní Ríain, Róisín 77
Northampton Saints 38
Northern Ireland football team 6, 9
Nottingham Forest 12, 18

O

O'Beirne, Mary 42
O'Brien, Aidan 57, 59
O'Brien, Anne 17
O'Brien, Vincent 59
O'Callaghan, Oisín 76
O'Callaghan, Pat 61
    Olympic Gold Medal (1928) 61
    Olympic Gold Medal (1932) 61
Ochigava, Sofya 53
O'Connell, Mick 31
O'Connell, Patrick (Don Patricio) 13
O'Connell, Paul 46
O'Connell, P.J. (Fingers) 33
O'Connor, Christy, Jr 81
O'Connor, Christy, Sr 81
O'Connor, Cian 64
O'Connor, Jamesie 33
O'Connor, Peter 70
    Olympic Silver Medal (1906) 70
O'Connor, William 85
O'Donovan, Gary 68
    Olympic Silver Medal (2016) 68
O'Donovan, Paul 68
    Olympic Silver Medal (2016) 68
O'Driscoll, Brian 38, 44, 46
O'Duffy Cup 22
O'Duffy, Sean 22
O'Dwyer, Mick 24, 30, 32
O'Gara, Ronan 40, 41, 44, 47
Olatunde, Israel 78
Old Trafford 12, 15
O'Leary, David 10
O'Loughlin, Sparrow 33
Olympic Aquatics 68
Olympic Flag 60
Olympic Games
    history of 60
    Ireland's Olympic History 61
    Irish Olympic Champions 61
    Nordic Games 65
    Summer Olympic Games 60, 65
    Winter Games 60, 65
Olympic Games (1904) (St Louis) 61, 71
Olympic Games (1906) (Athens) (Intercalated Games) 70
Olympic Games (1908) (London) 86
Olympic Games (1924) (Paris) 7, 61
Olympic Games (1928) (Amsterdam) 61
Olympic Games (1932) (Los Angeles) 61, 71
Olympic Games (1956) (Melbourne) 71, 75
Olympic Games (1984) (Los Angeles) 70
Olympic Games (1988) (Seoul) 52, 69
Olympic Games (1992) (Barcelona) 51, 52, 62, 69
Olympic Games (1996) (Atlanta) 69, 74
Olympic Games (2000) (Sydney) 63
Olympic Games (2004) (Athens) 51
Olympic Games (2008) (Beijing) 67
Olympic Games (2012) (London) 50, 53, 64, 69
Olympic Games (2016) (Rio) 66, 67, 68, 69, 82
Olympic Games (2020) (Tokyo) 53, 68, 82
Olympic Motto 60
O'Mahony, Danno 75
O'Mara, Frank 63
O'Neill, Martin 13
Original All Blacks (1905-6) 37
O'Rourke, Derval 63
Oscar Traynor Cup 7
Ó Sé, Páidí 30
O'Shea, Jack 32
O'Shea, John 12
O'Sullivan, Denise 17
O'Sullivan, Eddie 44
O'Sullivan, Marcus 63
O'Sullivan, Ronnie (The Rocket) 79, 84
O'Sullivan, Sonia 62–3
    Olympic Silver Medal (2000) 63
    World Championships Silver Medal 62
O'Toole, Olivia 14

P

Páirc Uí Chaoimh 53
Paralympics 66–7, 77
    London (2012) 66–7
    Rio (2016) 66
Parkes, James Cecil 86
    Australian Open (1912) 86
    Olympic Silver Medal (1908) 86
    Wimbledon (1914) 86
Parkhead Stadium, Glasgow 13
Parsons, Beibhinn 78
Pauw, Vera 8, 16
Peamount United 17, 18, 19
Peat, Lindsay 43
Pedroza, Eusebio 52
Peirce-Evans, Sophie Mary (Lady Heath) 61
Piggott, Lester 59
Poc Fada competition 26
Polo Grounds, New York 25
Premier League 12
    most Irish Premier League appearances 12
    red cards 12
    top Irish Premier League scorers 13
Premier League Hall of Fame 14
Purcell, Seán 31
Pušpure, Sanita 68

Q

Queensberry rules 48
Quinn, Niall 8, 11, 13

R

race walking 65
Ramsbottom, Sue 31
Ravenhill Roar 38
Ravenhill Stadium, Belfast 39
Real Betis 13
Reardon, Ray 84
Reid, T.J. 23
Republic of Ireland football team 6, 8
Rice, Lena 75
Ring, Christy 22, 29
road bowling 87
Robertson, Neil (The Thunder from Down Under) 84
Roche, Nicholas 73
Roche, Stephanie 17
    Puskás Award nomination 17
Roche, Stephen 73
    Giro d'Italia (1987) 73
    Tour de France victory (1987) 73
    World Championships (1987) 73
Rockmount AFC 12
Rohan, Mark 66
    Gold Medals (2012) 66
rounders 26, 27
rowing 68
RTÉ's soccer panel 14
rugby 36–7
    Connacht Rugby 38
    Dave Gallaher Trophy 37
    European Cup (2009) 38
    European Cup (2011) 38

greatest Irish players 46-7
Heineken Cup 39
history of rugby in Ireland 36
Leinster Rugby 38
Leinster Senior Cup 36
Munster Rugby 39
Munster Senior Cup 36
positions 37
positions by numbers 37
professional teams 36
schools 36
Ulster Rugby 39
Webb Ellis Trophy 36
World Rugby Hall of Fame 37
see also Irish International Rugby; Irish Women's Rugby
Rugby School 36
Rugby World Cup 42
Ryan, Eamonn 32
Ryder Cup 81, 82, 83

S

sailing 69
St James's Gate 18
St Mel's Park 19
St Patrick's Athletic FC 14, 18, 19
    Paddy the Panther (mascot) 19
Saipan 11
Sam Maguire Cup 21, 25, 30, 31, 79
Sampdoria 13, 14
Schillaci, Toto 10
Schmidt, Joe 41, 45
Scotland, shinty 26
Screeney, Adam 77
Second Irish International Soccer Match 7
Selby, Mark (The Jester from Leicester) 84
Setanta 26
Sexton, Johnny 38, 46
Shamrock Rovers 18, 19
    Hooperman (mascot) 19
Shankey, Maeve (Kyle) 75
Sheehy, Mikey 32
Shefflin, Henry (The King) 28, 33
Shelbourne (Shels) 18, 19
    Champions League (2004) 19
Sheridan, Martin 61
    Olympic Gold Medals 61
shinty 26
show jumping 86
    Aga Khan Cup 86
    World Championships 86
Six Nations 44, 45
Skibbereen Rowing Club 68
Sligo Rovers 18, 19
sliothar 23
Smith de Bruin, Michelle 69
    Olympic Gold Medals (1996) 69
Smith, James (Bonecrusher) 48
Smith, Rosemary 87
    Tulip Rally 87
Smyth, Jason 67
    Gold Medals 67
snooker 79, 84
    break in snooker 84
    Crucible Theatre, Sheffield 84
    maximum break 84
snooker nicknames 84
soccer 6-15, 78
    Athlone Town v AC Milan (1975) 19
    best European displays 19
    the Boys in Green 10, 11
    Champions League 19
    the Charlton years 10
    Europa League 19
    European Player of the Year (1968) 15

FAI Cup 14, 18, 47
first Irish international soccer match 7
Football Association of Ireland (FAI) 6, 7, 16
Girls in Green 16
'Granny Rule' 8
history of 6-7
Ireland's top scorers 11
Irish Clubs 19
Irish fans 9
Irish Football Association (IFA) 6, 7
Irish Premier League, most appearances 12
Irish Premier League, top scorers 13
Irish women's football team 16-17
League of Ireland 18-19
the Mick McCarthy era 11
Northern Ireland football team 9
Olé Olé Olé Olé! 8, 10
Premier League 12, 13
Premier League Hall of Fame 14
Puskás Award 17
'Put 'Em Under Pressure' 10
Red Cards 12
Republic of Ireland football team 8
Serie A (Italy) 13, 14
UEFA Cup 13
Women's National League 18
Soldier Field, Chicago 41, 45
Spanish Civil War 13
Spanish League 13
Special Olympic Games 69
Spillane, Pat 32
Sportsground, Galway 38
sprinting 78
Spurs 14
Stade de Reims 17
Stapleton, Frank 11
Stapleton, Nora 45
Staunton, Cora 30
Stringer, Peter 44
Stynes, Jim 27
swimming 77, 79
Szabo, Gabrielle 63

T

Taafe, Pat 56
Tailteann Games 61, 87
Taylor, Dennis 84
    World Championship (1985) 84
Taylor, Katie 50, 51, 53
    Olympic Gold Medal (2012) 53
Taylor, Pete 50
tennis
    Australian Open 86
    Irish players 61, 70, 75, 86
    Wimbledon 75, 86
Thomond Park, Limerick 39
Thunder and Lightning Final (1939) 23, 34
Tiedt, Fred 71
Timofte, Daniel 15
Tisdall, Bob 71
    Olympic Gold Medal (1932) 71
Tolka Park, Dublin 19
Tour de France 72-3
    Stephen Roche (1987) 73
Tour de France Femmes 72
Tour de France jerseys
    green jersey 72
    polka-dot jersey 72
    white jersey 72
    white on red number 72
    yellow jersey 72

Tracey, Larry 65
Traynor, Oscar 7
Treacy, John 63, 70
    Olympic Silver Medal (1984) 70
Treaty United FC 19
Trinity College Dublin 36
Trump, Judd (The Ace in the Pack) 84
Tuohy, Zach 27

U

UCD AFC 18, 19
UEFA Cup final 13
Ulster Rugby 39
    crest 39
    European Cup (1999) 39
    Heineken Cup 39
    Ravenhill (Kingspan Stadium) 39
Upton, Roisin 64

V

van Gerwen, Michael 85

W

Walsh, Katie 58
Walsh, Ruby 58
Walsh, Ted 58
Walsh, Tommy 33
Walters, Jonathan 13
War of Independence 24, 34
Ward, Tony 47
Waterford Football Club 19
Webb Ellis Trophy 36
Webb Ellis, William 36
Weld, Dermot 56
Wexford Football Club 19
Wexford Youths WFC 17, 18, 19
Whelahan, Brian 29
Whelan, Liam 8
Whiteside, Norman 9
Windsor Park, Belfast 9
Wolverhampton Wanderers 19
women's boxing 48, 50, 51, 53
    Hall of Fame 50
    Olympics (2012) 50
Women's National League 18
Women's Rugby Football Union 42
    Grand Slam (2013) 43
Women's Rugby World Cup (2014) 45
Wood, Keith 47
Woods, Tiger 83
World Cup (1958) (football) 9
World Cup (1966) (football) 10
World Cup (1982) (football) 9
World Cup (1986) (football) 9
World Cup (1987) (rugby) 41
World Cup (1990) (football) 10, 15
World Cup (1995) (rugby) 41
World Cup (2001) (football) 11
World Cup (2002) (football) 19
World Rugby Hall of Fame 37
World War I 37
World War II 7
wrestling 24, 75

Y

Yeats, Jack B.
    Liffey Swim, The (painting) 61
    Olympic Silver Medal (1924) 61

Z

Zenit Saint Petersburg 19

First published in Great Britain in 2023 by Red Shed, part of Farshore
An imprint of HarperCollins*Publishers*
1 London Bridge Street, London SE1 9GF
www.farshore.co.uk

HarperCollins*Publishers*
Macken House, 39/40 Mayor Street Upper
Dublin 1, D01 C9W8
Ireland

Text copyright © Adrian Russell
Illustrations copyright © Graham Corcoran
Adrian Russell and Graham Corcoran have asserted their moral rights.

Text layout by Sarah McCoy

ISBN 978-0-0086-4694-3
Printed in Italy
1

A CIP catalogue record for this title is available from the British Library.

All rights reserved. No part of this publication may be reproduced, stored in a retrieval system, or transmitted, in any form or by any means, electronic, mechanical, photocopying, recording or otherwise, without the prior permission of the publisher and copyright owner.

Stay safe online. Any website addresses listed in this book are correct at the time of going to print. However, Farshore is not responsible for content hosted by third parties. Please be aware that online content can be subject to change and websites can contain content that is unsuitable for children. We advise that all children are supervised when using the internet.

Farshore takes its responsibility to the planet and its inhabitants very seriously. We aim to use papers from well-managed forests run by responsible suppliers.